Confident, Sexy & Wildly free

How to own your worth, ditch
the self-doubt and not give a f*ck
what other people think of you

First published in 2021 by Nora Wendel

© Nora Wendel
The moral rights of the author have been asserted.
This book is a SpiritCast Network of Books

Author:

Wendel, Nora

Title:

Confident, Sexy & Wildly Free

ISBN:

9798666656242

Editor-in-chief: Cherise Lily Nana
Cover Design: Sarah Rose Graphic Design & Nora Wendel

Disclaimer:
The material in this publication is of the nature of general comment only, and does not represent professional advice. It is not intended to provide specific guidance for particular circumstances and it should not be relied on as the basis for any decision to take action or not take action on any matter which it covers. Readers should obtain professional advice where appropriate, before making any such decision. To the maximum extent permitted by law, the author and publisher disclaim all responsibility and liability to any person, arising directly or indirectly from any person taking or not taking action based on the information in this publication.

To Her

Every day;
It's me I wake up to.

My skin still hugging me tightly even though I didn't ask for any love.
My heart still swirling all alone on the dance floor because it didn't give up on me.

It's not me I pray to, soft whispers of words on my lips.
My devotion rising and falling in love with you, not me.

And

Every day it's me I wake up to but it's not me I dream about, eyes flirting with the imagined reality of your beauty before me.

Every day;
It's me I wake up to.
And yet, it's not me I long for.

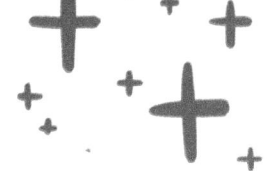

Stop. Breathe.
You are here.

I was exactly where you are.

I had this deep yearning, this inner longing for more. My anxiety was crippling me. WHAT WAS MY PURPOSE? Why couldn't I just be 'normal' like that woman over there [insert a woman you can't keep your eyes off in a coffee shop or that woman you see on your Instagram feed whose profile you spend 30 minutes scrolling down, tapping on each and every photo, devouring her life].

'Normal' to me was a woman who had it all together; her friends loved her, she had a big mission driving her forward in life, her business was thriving, she had her beloved. She had purpose, she had what I wanted. *So why didn't I have that?*

What was wrong with me?

I'm writing this book because I became that woman that I couldn't take my eyes off. Today passion oozes from my pores, joy is my password for life and being an inspiration is my purpose.

How did that happen? What got me from hiding, feeling scared, listless and unsatisfied with my life to being a confident, sexy and wildly free woman?

The HOW is what this book is about.

This isn't just a book. I don't 'just' do the norm.

This is a PLAYBOOK.
A chance for you to rip off the constrictions of your mind and run naked through life, going, *"Fuck me, is this what freedom feels like? Gimme more of THIS, please, universe!"*

Ah yes. Freedom. I'll be sharing more about the meaning we give freedom in the first few chapters, but for now, let me whisper in your ear ...

"Are you ready?"

Are you ready to join me as I unravel my own journey with you?

The reason I call this a playbook is because I'm taking you through my own processes, tools and mindset shifts. It's really not a *read-and-put-down-and-forget-about-it kind of book.*

I want your pen to hit your journal running out of ink, I want tears to be streaming down your face as you realise THE reason you keep sabotaging yourself, I want sighs of sweetness to ripple through your being as you learn what true self-compassion feels like.

I want all that for you and more. In order for that to happen, I need to ask you about your level of commitment.

You picked up this book because something resonated with you.

Perhaps it was a feeling of discontentment with your life.
Perhaps it was an inner knowing that there is more to your life.
Perhaps you have hit the point of having enough of feeling shitty, clamouring to get out of the negative Nancy hug of your mind, who has trapped you in her smothering embrace.

You want to learn how you can feel confident, sexy and wildly free with yourself.

And that, my love, is what I'm here to guide you on. I can only guide you if you are willing to be led. Effortless is my word and I'm sure as hell not going to be pushing and shoving you from behind as you scratch me, screaming, "Stop it, stop it."

That's not effortless.

I'm revving my big, black, sexy 225cc custom Honda motorbike parked in your driveway, helmet for you in one hand, smiling and asking you, *"Are you coming along for the ride?"*

'Cause if you are, we're going to swim into wild waterfalls, run along the rice paddies, sip coconuts at my favourite vegan cafe whilst giggling at how great our life is. Why? How?

Because you get to CHOOSE life to be this great.

Want that? Read on.

There are journalling questions, meditations, affirmations, emotional freedom technique (tapping) videos and so much more that this playbook contains, all with the single purpose of teaching you how to own your worth, ditch the self-doubt and not give a f*ck what other people think of you.

Do. the. Playwork.

It's not homework, 'cause who likes homework?!
It's PLAYwork, 'cause you get a chance to play with who you want to become; THAT IS EXCITING! CAN YOU TELL HOW EXCITED I AM FOR YOU?

Ultimately, this is a journey for you to feel GREAT about yourself and your life.

Are you willing to take the risk to feel great?

Get out the lipstick, put on that sexy lingerie, do YOU to the max, 'cause this shiz is about to get real: real fun, real deep, real freeing.

And I'm here with you drying your tears, giving you big hugs and whispering in your ear, "You are so much more amazing than you think you are."

Xo
Nora

PS There is no wrong way to do this book, your feelings are valid, your experiences are valid, you get to do you.

I do *suggest* you read the book all in one go and then go back chapter by chapter and do the playwork. This means you get to read in one beautiful flow and get your mind to start thinking about your life. Then when you go back you can take your time answering each of the journalling questions. The work is in the journalling questions as this is when you can apply it to YOUR LIFE. Even if you have done some of the playwork before; approach this like a child in another child's toy room—eyes wide open, full of wonder and awe at all this STUFF to play with!

PPS I'd get a brand-new journal for this playwork. I just love having a fresh, clean journal to start diving deep into my thoughts, plus plenty of space to just scrawl all my 'me-ness' over!

PPPS You can find all the extra digital playwork on my website under www.norawendel.com/confidentsexyfree

PPPPS This is just the start of it all. I go even deeper into all of this in my online courses and group coaching programs. Check out my website to find out more!

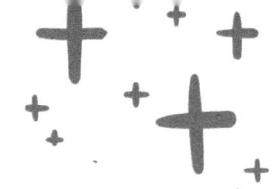

table of contents

introduction

I wasn't okay.

I felt my internal heat rising; scrambling, I quickly tried to untie the wool scarf wrapped around my neck to get some fresh air. I ripped my headphones off my ears as the pounding psytrance faded away. I heard the beeping warning of the doors closing and I knew—I HAD TO GET OUT. I stumbled onto the platform as the tube doors shut behind me and the train started moving.

I still wasn't okay.

I undid my thick winter coat, panicking and feeling things I'd never felt before: fear, death, heart pumping. I turned and ran up the escalators. I needed fresh air NOW.

~

I was 24, studying art at university in London and I had just had my first panic attack on the London Underground during the morning rush hour. That was the start of my journey. That was the start of my mistrust, distrust and deep-rooted fear that *I was not okay.*

It has taken me just under 10 years to feel more than okay again, to feel radiant, to trust the universe, to feel

the self-compassion and ever-greater rising love of life emanating from my being.

For the majority of my 20s and early 30s I was a deeply fearful woman. The undertone of anxiety was the only norm in my life. The constant fear that I wasn't okay, that I couldn't do big things, that I couldn't do things ALONE. Going from codependent relationship (I couldn't be alone now, could I? My anxiety would come back!) to codependent relationship (yes, I moved from Australia to Brazil, and New Delhi, India to Cape Town, all for men).

There was a quality of unsatisfactoriness to my life. I didn't know my greater purpose and I longed to know. I couldn't plan my goals for fear of not being successful. I couldn't decide where I wanted to be, it always seemed 'better' over there! Hence I moved from my university in London to another university in Australia, then to Brazil, then to India and then to Cape Town, finally settling in Bali.

My anxiety didn't stop me from travelling; I grew up as a global gypset girl, being born in Thailand, raised in Nepal, boarding school in India, Mum and Dad in separate Asian countries. Travelling was the norm for me; however, I dreaded it. Hated it. Feared what would happen if I got a panic attack again. I didn't feel safe in my own body; *I didn't feel safe being me.*

I didn't get better on my own, I had loads of help along the way. When I first had my panic attack and I wasn't okay, my mum recommended I try EFT tapping therapy in London to be able to get back onto the bus (I had severe anxiety being in any spaces where I couldn't control getting on or off myself), the help didn't stop there, I got counselling in every country I lived in, I did Gurdjieff dance therapy in Goa, India for 10 weeks. I remember the tears of joy when on the final day of performance I didn't have a freaking clue what I was doing (i.e. I didn't know the next moves) and when in the taxi ride home Pharrell Williams' song 'Happy' came on, and I burst into such a big smile as I realised I WAS OKAY NOT KNOWING! That was a first step towards healing my internal terror of needing to be in control the whole time.

In Bali I had weekly sessions with a psychotherapist; I also dived deep into feminine embodiment practices guided by the many amazing coaches/healers/movers living in Ubud so I could reconnect to my body, the body which had failed me when I had that panic attack, the body which I didn't trust.

I trained in Authentic Relating as I knew connection and community was a way I did feel safe around people and ultimately myself especially when I knew how to express my deepest fears and be held in a non-judgmental space.

I learnt leadership techniques on retreats to regain the feeling of empowerment. It felt good. It felt great.

I did the work as I wasn't willing to be this woman who felt stuck, who felt limited by her own fears, who just wasn't happy with herself deep down.

It was about eight years into my anxiety journey when my best friend suggested that I go and do Landmark Forum as another tool to shed any stories I had about who I was or could be. Landmark Forum is a transformational three-day boot camp aimed at self-realisation around the stories or lies you tell yourself. Totally my kind of personal development!

And yet ... the thing was that the next training I wanted to do was in Sydney. It meant I had to fly there alone. Shit.

I didn't feel like I could do it.

Still after ALL these years. I didn't trust myself that I was going to be okay.

I knew I needed more help. I had heard of NLP (Neuro-Linguistic Programming) over the years and I had my inner intuition telling me that finding a NLP coach would help me.

I was at the Saturday organic market in Ubud where I was living at the time when I ran into Chad, a friend who I knew from Cape Town.

"How you doing?" he asked.
"Pretty shitty," I replied. (I am not one for pretending and glazing over true emotions, something I learnt in Authentic Relating.)

"Oh, tell me more." He opened the space between us for more of a connection.

"I'm feeling stuck and low about myself, I really want to go to Landmark Forum in Sydney next month and I just don't feel like I can. I've been thinking of doing some NLP to help me, do you know anyone?" I asked him.

"I do," he replied. "I have this amazing Indian lady I have been working with for 10 years or so, I'll pass you her contact. Give her a WhatsApp."

It turns out that Reena Jabran was the last seed that planted my most luscious and fragrant rose garden. She got me on that Bali to Sydney flight in under two weeks of NLP therapy with her. I did Landmark Forum ALONE, not knowing anyone, and even stayed in an Airbnb around the corner from the venue (something that brought up such fear in me before).

I felt proud.
F YES, I DID IT!

I was radiating.

I was empowered.

I ended up working with Reena for a year and a half in online weekly sessions before flying to India (yes, alone!) and training as an NLP practitioner with her in early 2020.

I no longer have chronic low level anxiety.
I no longer majorly doubt myself.
I no longer want to stay small out of fear.
I no longer lack purpose.
I no longer feel worthless.

I have a set of tools, I have a set of processes, I have trained in Feminine Embodiment, Authentic Relating, Transformational Leadership, NLP and most importantly, I have *the experience of what it feels like* to be shy, hating myself, totally disconnected, and constantly in doubt and fear of my own life.

What is the opposite of that then?

What's the opposite of lack of self-worth, constant self-doubt, and overcaring what people think of you?

It's a woman who deeply knows her values, has her boundaries, loves who she is, feels sexy from the inside out, is so secure in herself that she doesn't need the external validation from others and isn't afraid to speak her truth.

No more people pleasing.
No more thinking she can't have it all.
No more feeling small.
No more perpetuating self-doubt keeping her from taking inspired action.

She is a woman who is confident, sexy and wildly free, and you are going to become her.

THERE IS NOTHING WORSE THAN BECOMING A WATERED DOWN VERSION OF SOMEONE ELSE.

chapter 1
what do you want?

"How do I become her?" you ask. "That confident, sexy and wildly free version of myself?"

That, my love, is my genius ability. I teach Feminine Magnetism: the art of being a confident and sexy woman in love with herself and her life. How would you describe a Magnetic Woman? You guessed it ...

It's the woman who turns heads when she walks into any space, not because of her external beauty but because of how she carries herself.

It's the woman on the dance floor with the biggest smile on her face as she just lets loose without any hindrance to her self-expression or care at looking silly or weird or uncoordinated. She just is freely herself.

It's the woman you can't help but keep looking at, being reeled in by her vibe. "More," you say to yourself. "I want more of THAT."

It's the woman who you want to be friends with, to hang out with, to be around ALL the time.

A magnetic woman is a woman who owns her worth, doesn't settle for anything but her biggest desires, believes she can have it all, has the passion and purpose in her life so that she constantly takes inspired action, knows she is the 'hot shit', and yet has the biggest, kindest heart full of compassion and empowers everyone around her so that THEY feel great.

She is empowered and she empowers.

Yum. Yes.

~

YOUR POTENTIAL IS ENDLESS

If that is a magnetic woman, how do you get to BEING her? Read on, love, read on.

There is a reason you aren't her yet.

There are fears, stories, beliefs and past experiences stopping you from embodying her, and this is where we are going to start the unravelling together.

I'm going to ask you two questions: these two questions had me trembling back in my anxiety days as I really had no idea about the answers, so I'm going to guide you to dig a little deeper. Remember there is no wrong way to do this. Your desires are valid, your fears are valid, your experiences are valid.

And in case you are freaking out inside, *you can change your desires at any time.*

It was one of my big fears. "Oh, I want to live in India (BUT what if I don't anymore?)"; that push and pull with my desires led to inaction in my life and it was a debilitating feeling that caused internal frustration and such self-hate in my life. Now I tell myself, "Right now I want this AND it's okay to change what I want at any time." Ah, relief! Reframing it that way feels so much better to me. The whole point of this book is to get you to FEEL GREAT about yourself.

Here's how to do this first journalling playwork:

Take out a pen and your journal and turn on some fast-paced music and set a timer for 10 minutes. Don't let your pen leave the paper for ALL that time. Keep writing, even if you don't know what to write, write: "This is stupid, I don't know what to write." The aim of this is to get your conscious mind out of the way (by not stopping writing) and allow your subconscious mind to surface with its desires ...

Got it?
Here you go ...

journalling question
What do I want?

Journalling on this question may bring up paralysing doubt, lack of self-worth and internal fear: "I can't have the $250K-a-year business"; "Who am I to want two kids AND a thriving business AND live in Bali?"

That's the point of getting you to write down your desires—not the desires you feel 'good enough' for right now, I want the big, juicy desires that make your insides fill with butterflies because 'what if that were possible?'

I want those desires.

Go back and add to your journalling if you didn't allow yourself to dream bigger. (Maybe it didn't feel safe; I'll address that later on in this book.)

Looking at your list of desires, think about WHY you want them. This is an important part of the process and one of the foundations of this book.

Everything we want in life is to feel a certain way.

We are not only Human Beings we are Human FEELINGS. We navigate life according to how we feel or want to feel. (Understanding this is also the secret to becoming a manifesting queen)

Everything you want is because you think you will feel a certain way when you have it.
And that feeling is usually thinking you will feel 'better' by having that.

For example, I wanted a custom motorbike here in Bali because I knew I would feel like a sexy badass on it. I didn't *need* the motorbike to feel sexy and like a badass, I could just decide that I wanted to feel sexy and like a badass and embody that. However, since we have been taught to associate material objects with feelings, we think when we have *that*, then we can feel *this*. That's a false premise that I want you to examine deeply in your life and what this journalling playwork in this chapter is all about.

Go back to your list of desires. On a new journal page draw a line down the middle so you have two columns. On the left write down your list of desires. On the right write down *why* you want it (i.e. how it will make you feel having it).

In my example:

Desire   **Reason WHY**
Custom motorbike   To feel like a sexy badass

Our feelings are our driving force in life and most of the time we aren't aware of the deeper reasons WHY we want something, it just 'seems' like it'll make us happy/ give us status/make us feel freer. Understanding the feeling reason underneath your desires will allow you to stop living your life on autopilot and instead become the conscious creatress of your life. Feelings are important; start observing your feelings from this moment forward so you can practise being highly self-aware. It'll only lead to more greatness in your life.

~

Moving on to the second journalling question. Use the same 10-minute journalling hack I outlined above: pen hits the paper for 10 minutes non-stop. Allow whatever wants to come out to just come out.

journalling question
Who do I want to be?

Let me give you some more guidance on this question. What does the ultimate version of you feel? How does she act? (her behaviours) What are her habits? How does she relate to herself?

Go and let loose, pen to paper.

~

Done? Great!

Now we have a clearer vision of both what you desire in your life (it's allowed to be material and non-material, FYI) and who you want to be. This is juicy stuff right here, it's like the hunk of marble before it gets chiselled into the most gorgeous Greek goddess statue, i.e. YOU!

Looking back at your scribbles of desires and the reason WHY you want them, we are going to add another layer to this. I now want you to list:

- Why you don't have that yet
- Why you think you can't have that

- Why you feel like you can't be that woman already

Journalling on this will bring up all your stories, lies and limiting beliefs. Don't despair. This is exactly what we want to have access to—the inner workings of your brain! You are getting a clearer and clearer internal look at:

A. What you desire
B. Who you want to be
C. Your beliefs and thoughts that are stopping you from getting it/becoming her

This journalling playwork is showing you the exact reasons why you don't have what you want in life! Congrats, you just dived headfirst into your own internal jungle. Perhaps you were walking down a little dirt path covered with vines and spiderwebs, having no idea where you were going, when suddenly you discovered a clearing with a magnificent waterfall whose banks were covered in the most beautiful flowers; you feel relief, you feel joy, you can't wait to strip down to go for a refreshing swim. That's what I feel like whenever I do this journalling playwork.

By the way, this isn't a one-off journalling exercise. I still do this in my journal often, at least once a month. It's a constant checking in with myself around what I think I can or cannot have and who I think I can or cannot be.

Stop shrinking to fit into places you've outgrown

The fact is we can have anything
we want and be whoever we want
to be.

Why don't we go for it in life then?
What has us doubting, fearing, staying small?

This is where it gets really interesting and I'm about to nerd out on some (simplified) neuroscience with you.

Our limiting beliefs, our fears, or what I call our negative Nancys are what is keeping us from having everything we want (as you saw in your own journalling, right?). All these are simply THOUGHTS pinging around our brain. What do thoughts and the brain have to do with being a confident, sexy woman?

Stay with me here.

The brain has two main functions:

1. To keep us alive aka SAFE (turn us away from pain) and
2. To keep the body in balance by optimising energy consumption

Makes sense so far.

Let me ask you, how does the brain know what is 'safe'? What instruction manual is it operating on to understand what safe is and what danger is? Who is telling it what to do?

The brain's operating manual is PAST EXPERIENCE, and past experience are stored as your memories. More specifically, memories associated with feelings we internalised.

Everything we experience leaves a feeling residue that is either 'feel good, more of this, please' or 'feel bad, don't want to feel this again'. The feel-good feelings aren't of much concern to us right now. It's the feel-bad feelings that trigger the response in the brain to think, "Is this a threat to our survival? Yes? YES?! Okay, make note, that experience isn't safe for us."

The Brain Works on the Past

Anytime you get out of your comfort zone, i.e. wanting to stretch yourself to get your desires, your brain scans your memories of past experiences and starts hitting the PANIC NOW button as it learns you haven't ever done anything like this before, so it MUST BE UNSAFE.

RETREAT. RETREAT. Flight, fright or freeze activated. Your survival is at risk!

Go back to the comfort zone. It's safe there. Out there with that big scary goal, oh no, that's not safe!

Can you understand why we cognitively understand our goals and yet it seems so hard to actually achieve them, especially if they are wayyy up there and stretching ourselves?

When I really understood this I had such self-compassion.

"Oh Nora, all your sabotaging, niggling, itty bitty shitty committee just means you care so deeply about yourself! You want to stay alive. I get you. I understand you." That is how I started talking to myself instead of self-hating and getting more and more frustrated at WHY THE F WASN'T I ABLE TO JUST GET ON THE PLANE AGAIN?!

Remember my experience of anxiety was a huge life experience that caused me pain (the panic in my body). I remembered that experience as something I didn't enjoy. It was associated with travelling, so my brain made the association that all travel was potentially life threatening and therefore even a thought of travelling alone would trigger similar bodily feelings of panic and anxiety even though I KNEW that this was a different situation.

Ah, brain. I love you so dearly! You are just trying to protect me.

Start saying this to yourself whenever you notice self-sabotage or internal frustration at not moving forward, and you'll shift the feelings from self-hate to self-appreciation, and that feels like such relief.

I want you to think of some life experiences you've had that you categorised as 'not good feeling' or of causing pain and note how similar situations cause the same feelings to surface and how you retreat back into 'safety'. Just make a note; it's more than likely that this is a way you sabotage yourself. More about self-sabotage in Chapter 2.

Let's talk about the second function of the brain: conserving energy.

Some of our beliefs are just a tedious wet spaghetti mess that we can't seem to get a grip on.

Can you relate to this?

Surely I can just 'believe' that I am worthy enough to ask for the sale with the potential new client? So why am I freaking the F out, sweating, feeling so undeserving and fearing rejection so badly that I just don't do it? Then I feel even more shit, berate myself for not being confident enough, self-flagellate, cry some and decide online business is not for me.

Why does my belief that I can't ask for what I want/ am not worthy enough stop me?

The answer lies in the fact that rewiring a belief takes effort. The brain doesn't like effort, it likes ease, it likes effortlessness; thinking a new thought takes more effort than allowing the old thought pattern to flow. The result is, we often revert back to old ways of thinking (beliefs) that don't serve us anymore in getting our new desires or becoming that new version of ourselves.

Our brains are just doing their jobs—keeping us alive and safe and conserving energy. Words of advice from a chronic self-hater: stop *hating* on yourself so much, okay? There is nothing *wrong* with you.

All we have to do is dig a little deeper, uncover more of your thoughts and unravel them to show yourself that you are safe, that you have got this, and that the big bold life you want to live is right there waiting for you.

You've started the unravelling in this chapter; don't stop now, it really does get better and better.

Before moving on I also want to mention that a lot of our life is ruled by subconscious programs. Subconscious programs are ideas/stories/beliefs that we aren't even aware of but they govern how we act out every day.

For example, I really want to wear my white pair of cute jeans shorts and yet I never do. They sit in my cupboard neatly folded waiting for the day they get to feel my skin. I may have a subconscious program based on a memory (that I can't remember!) that my dad once told me that white shorts didn't look good on me and I should go and change clothes. This memory translates into me never feeling comfortable wearing the jeans shorts EVEN THOUGH I really want to and I know they look great on me!

Don't get scared. You may be thinking, "This is a lot to take in. I want so much (my desires) and I want it to feel a certain (good) way. My brain isn't letting me get what I want because of my thoughts and now there are things that I don't even know about that are stopping me too?! Do I have any hope?"

Yes, you do. Vast, glittering rainbows of hope, in fact. This book is guiding you to uncover more and more of those silly stories you tell yourself, whether you are aware of them or not. You are here and that shows that you are willing to take a deeper look at yourself right now and what you have or do not have in your life.

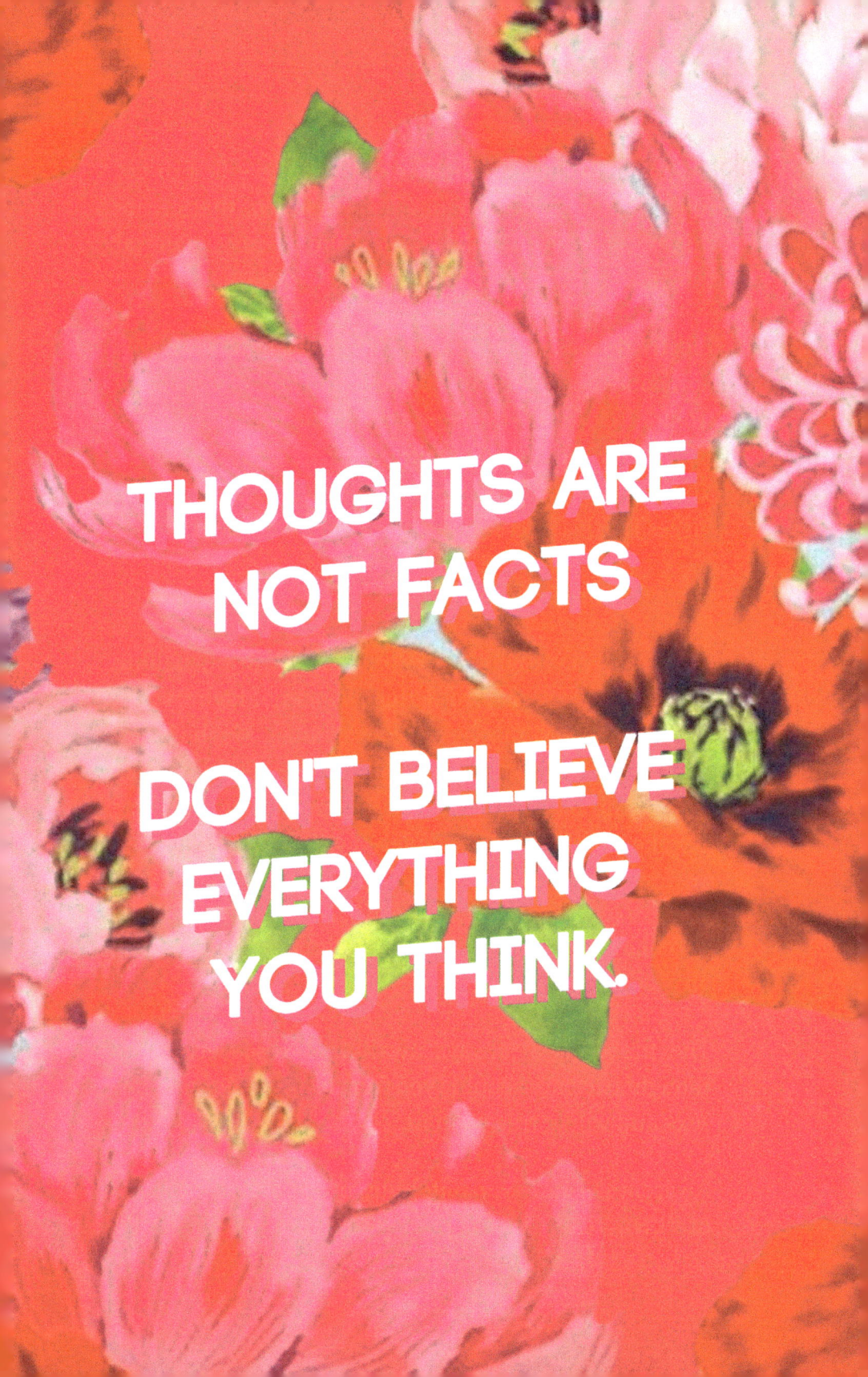

Everything that you do have or don't have is a direct reflection of your thoughts. It is thoughts that create things. An idea (which is a thought) creates material things.

Electricity was made from the idea (thought) of it.
Someone once had the idea to make sexy lingerie (thank f*ck for that, I don't want to be wearing granny panties for the rest of my life!).
Your computer was once a thought (even all the little pieces inside the computer were once a thought too!)

Thought creates things.

Take a look at your life and go back to the two journalling playwork questions from this chapter. Maybe you'll add some notes, maybe you'll rearrange. Maybe you'll ponder over this in your candlelit rose petal lavender bath bomb bath tonight. Tag me on Instagram if you do take a bath—@norawendel—I want to share in your self-care delight!

"Do I have any hope?" You ask again! Yes you do. Keep on reading.

The first step is always awareness, discovering the thoughts that are keeping you from being that confident, sexy and wildly free woman.

Awareness is an ever-unfolding process, that's the joy of it! No, really, that *is* the joy of it. We are constantly yearning to thrive, to grow, to be better, do better. Not the 'I'm not good enough, need to self-hate and add to my list of shoulds' kind of better, I'm talking about the 'I freaking ROCK and want to continue to rock' kind of better.

Okay, this was a lot of 'heady' stuff in this chapter right here. It was all mindset based. What you think matters. How you talk to yourself matters. THOUGHTS REALLY DO CONTROL YOUR REALITY.

Become hyperaware of your thoughts. Examine them. Praise them if they are moving you forward in growth, reexamine them if they are keeping you small. Become your own scientific experiment. Ask yourself—are these thoughts serving me?

Is this what my ideal confident, sexy and free self would think?

Let that question be your guiding question from now on.

~

In this chapter we dived into your desires, understood the feeling reason why you want what you want. We learnt how FEELINGS are the basis of how we navigate life and understood that our brain loves us deeply even though it seems like the opposite. Reminder: more self-compassion, less self-hate!

The next chapter is all about finding out the biggest story (lie) we tell ourselves, seeing *how* we sabotage and how our needy inner children are throwing temper tantrums in our adult lives without us even realising it. It's time to claim back our own power, hug our inner children and stake claim to our desires.

you are
busy doubting
yourself when
other people
are intimidated
by your
potential.

chapter 2
our needy inner children

Chapter one was all about getting clear on what we want and who we want to be. Realising that **thought** controls us—either in a positive way (yay! I achieved my goal!) or then stopping us getting what we want (hey, there, negative Nancy!). In this chapter we will be understanding how to become the conscious creatress of our lives, learning what self sabotage is and giving love to the unmet emotional needs of our inner child(ren).

How are our thoughts formed? Are we just born with our minds filled with our can'ts and shoulds and 'yes, that is okay to do' or 'no, you can't do that'? You know this isn't true if you think back to you from 10 years ago; you don't think the *exact* same thoughts now as you did then (*some* maybe, but not all). We live life and our experience of life changes us, we adapt according to our goals and external circumstances, we take on new stories based on our experiences and whether they were good or bad, and we form new ideas about ourselves and who we think we can be all because we live this thing called life. How amazing! Why aren't we

living that confident, sexy and free life we dream about then?

It has to do with understanding how thought is formed in our minds and continuing to understand how thought forms our beliefs and stories.

Thoughts are formed by external influence, meaning everything in our external environment that is largely uncontrollable to us. (I say largely because we can control our immediate surroundings like our home, friends, etc., and larger than that is out of our control.)

It's through *our senses* that we filter in the external environment and it's through our senses that we start to form thought. Remember when I shared thoughts create reality? Here's how it works:

External influence is filtered through our senses to form thought. A thought you keep thinking forms a belief. We have multiple beliefs about ourselves and our lives which make up our belief system (what we think we can or cannot do); our belief system governs our behaviour (I can do that, I can't do that), which leads to the type of action or inaction we take. The actions we do or don't take create the reality that you see in front of you in the mirror every day.

Mind blowing, I know.

Here it is mapped out in a simpler way:

External influence = Thoughts = Beliefs (+ Belief System) = Behaviour (Action) = Our Reality

If you follow on from this and have the desire to change your reality because you are unhappy, unsatisfied and longing for more, and it's reflected in a job you hate, a body you loathe and crumbling relationships, *what do you need to work on?* (Remember, you can't change your external influence to an extent.) **What you can change is the way you think.**

In order to change the way you think you have to look at when and how your first thoughts were formed.

The Importance of Childhood

Let's go back to the beginning of our lives, empty vessels of pure bliss and joy, I like to call our baby selves. Language is still being formed, life is all new, wondrous and to be explored. Who is informing and influencing us as babies? Our main caretakers, which for most of us are our parents. We **depend** on our parents to take care of our survival in our early lives, we have no other choice; it's them and what they offer us, or death. As children we need a) basic survival as food + shelter b) care and attention and c) love and validation. When any of these are not given or lacking, we start to internalise feelings of unworthiness, doubt or neediness, etc.

When you look at it this way you can see how we easily take on our main caretakers' beliefs, stories, judgments and general way of life because our caretakers are our sole source of survival; our identity is formed based off what we know (i.e. the world of our caretakers). In order to start to change the way we think we need to acknowledge our childhood and the experiences which shaped us.

Our experiences of childhood are carried with us through the rest of our lives, often unconsciously controlling us (self-sabotage) until we become aware of them and then *consciously* choose a different story to tell.

The second most important question I ask all my clients after "What do you desire and why?" is:

What happened in your childhood that made you think you aren't worthy/that it is not safe to share/that you can't be whoever you want to be?

Let that sink in for a minute. It's a big question (one which you will be answering later on in this chapter). I'm asking you to look back at your childhood and allow for those experiences which you don't want to remember to come up again. Our childhood goes on for years; you can't possibly remember *everything,* right? Totally true, and I'm not asking you to spend weeks meticulously remembering your childhood over the years.

I can guarantee you there is a memory from your childhood where you were shamed, told off, sent away, talked down to, dismissed, ignored, bullied and so forth, *for just being you.* From this experience you have then formed a (false) belief that it's not okay to be that way.

It's not okay to share my voice (because I'll be told off for screaming too loud).
It's not okay to wear what I want (because I'll be sent to my room for wearing Mum's best diamond earrings which I then lost).
It's not okay to ask for help in class (because the smart girl at school will tease me and bully me).
It's not okay to ask questions (because the one time I did I got slapped as Dad said it was rude).

Can you see the correlation? The experience you had as a child where you wanted validation, love and encouragement turned to a 'bad feeling' with consequences where it didn't feel safe or it didn't feel okay to be you; therefore, you created the story (essentially a thought repeated over and over again) that you couldn't share your voice because there was a bad consequence (feeling) related to that. The brain then categorised this whole experience as a potential threat to survival and as a painful experience to be avoided hence **any other experience remotely similar** to the one from your childhood will trigger that same limiting belief/story and your brain will do everything it can to stop you experiencing that same feeling.

Fast forward to your life today. You want to walk into a room and own yourself, proud and womanly and full of self-love, yet at the same time you feel like you can't even post a selfie of you on Facebook with a truthful caption. You don't understand why you feel so shy, so unworthy, so lacking in confidence. It seems scary. "That'll never be me," you tell yourself as you see other women sharing so openly. You stay small, you stay hiding, secretly longing to be that woman who turns heads with just her energy.

Ask yourself, what happened in my childhood where I had an experience of owning myself and sharing truthfully that turned into a painful emotional experience? Dig up that memory and write it down.

The majority of your limiting beliefs come from a childhood experience and they are ruling your adult life causing serious obstructions to who you want to be and what you want to have.

It's time to love up your inner child so we can move past those silly stories holding you back.

Grab the tissues; the first time I did this playwork I bawled. In fact, this morning in my meditation the tears were there as I told my inner child how much I loved her and was so proud of her!

GRATEFUL
THANKFUL
GRATEFUL
THANKFUL
GRATEFUL
THANKFUL
GRATEFUL
THANKFUL

It's Not Their Fault

I want you to recognise that a lot of, *if not most*, self-sabotage is happening in your life because you have an emotionally starved temper-tantrum-throwing inner child who wants attention and validation for their existence and didn't get what they wanted! Cue eye roll here; we know what a child's temper tantrum is like, right?

Let me make it clear that you could have had the most loving childhood with the most adoring caretakers and still have internalised stories of not being lovable, not being worthy, or feeling a threat to your safety. The fact is that you interpreted a situation where one of your needs may not have been met the way **YOU** wanted it to be met and then created the story that sticks with you for life.

As I shared above, as children we have needs, from basic such as survival (food, shelter) to more complicated emotional needs (love, feeling validated in our existence). *It's the unmet emotional needs that lead to internalised feelings of lack of worthiness or feelings of being unlovable.*

Ultimately we all desire to be seen, heard and appreciated for who we are. When any one of those is negated in childhood we create stories and beliefs around what we experienced that simply aren't true.

For example, I really wanted the emotional attention of my dad when I was nine. I wanted him to hug me and tell me how proud of me he was. When that didn't happen, I internalised that I had to do better, be better, in order for him to be proud of me, leading to me creating a story that I am not good enough as I am.

Another example: You could be two years old, not having language formed properly, sitting in your high chair at the table, screaming your head off, wanting the attention of your mum who is busy preparing food for you (unknown to you). She doesn't come for another ten minutes during which you created a story for yourself that you don't deserve love.

Yes, it really can be as simple as that.

I'm going to point out this isn't your parents' fault. I didn't write this so you get to blame your parents for the way you are. That's not personal empowerment. Forgive them, they were doing the best they knew how with all their stories and beliefs playing out in their heads.

Playwork: Forgive your parents
Close your eyes, think of your mum (or one of your primary caregivers) and repeat this: I'm sorry, please forgive me, I thank you, I love you.

Now do the same for your dad (or one of your other primary caregivers).

Great! We have stopped the external blame and now we can go back to empowering ourselves. I'm a big believer in integrating the unmet emotional needs from our inner child in adulthood so that they stop causing reactive patterns of self-sabotage. In order to integrate the unmet emotional needs we need to a) find out what they are and b) welcome them with so much love.

Finding Out Your Unmet Emotional Needs From Childhood

Looking back over the limiting beliefs you journalled from Chapter 1, I want you to spend some time going back to your childhood and remembering experiences and events that created the same feelings of not being safe, not being okay, feeling ashamed for being you, etc.

It's time for that flower petal lavender bath bomb self-care activity again. Or if baths aren't your thing, perhaps a long walk in nature with your dog, or quietly sipping your coffee in the early hours of the morning when you have time and space to be you and think.

This journalling question may take more than just a few minutes to think about. It's asking you to go into your past; it may be scary, you may have blocked it out.

I'm asking you to be gentle with yourself as you slowly pry open each petal lovingly.

journalling question

What happened in my childhood that I started to believe these limiting beliefs?

You may have a list looking something like this:

Desire: To post whatever I want on Instagram/ Facebook

Belief: No one will listen to what I have to say, I'll be rejected

Childhood experience: At one of my parents' home parties I wanted to sing my favourite song and my parents weren't having any of it and told me to go and play in my room alone. I felt rejected and spent the rest of the evening in my room feeling lonely.

Keep going down your list of desires and beliefs, adding on the childhood experience and if you remember the age you were as well. What you'll end up with is a clearer idea of where these silly stories you tell yourself came from.

It's also okay if you don't remember. Be kind to yourself. Tell yourself you'll remember when the time is right and move on to the next one; we are staying away from the self-hate here.

This list you just created will show you what your childhood emotional needs were. Maybe you really wanted to be listened to. Maybe you wanted hugs from your parents. Maybe you wanted to hear the words "I'm so proud of you". **Whatever you wanted was and is still valid.**

Let's give your little girl exactly what she wanted, okay?

It's time to go and download my inner child meditation #1. It's 15 minutes long and you are going to be welcoming in all your inner children (the you from baby up to teenager) and giving them all so much love.

Playwork: Do the inner child meditation #1
You can find the Playwork here:
www.norawendel.com/confidentsexyfree

After doing the inner child meditation #1, I suggest journalling what came up and practising some self-care (bath, walk, tea, book, whatever makes you come back to yourself). You may have bawled your eyes out (I did the first time!) or you may have felt resistance to doing this. It's all okay. You can revisit this inner child meditation at any time in your life; your inner child at whatever age will never say no to being loved by you! Inner child meditation #1 is the first stage of integrating the unmet emotional needs of your little girl. It's about welcoming her in all her stages of development.

If this is the first time you have done any inner child playwork, meditation #1 will be a powerful experience; make sure you allow full integration of what you just went through before moving on to the next meditation. I usually suggest a few days (three or more) of practising loving all your inner children in all the ages.

If you have done inner child playwork before then you can move directly on to meditation #2 the following day.

Keep watering yourself

You're growing

-E.Russel

Inner child meditation #2

Inner child meditation #2 goes deeper and asks you to call forth *one* of your inner children at a specific age (you get to decide which age and any age you bring forth is the perfect age). This is the inner child that is most needy, that feels the most unloved, that feels the most unworthy. Perhaps there is a certain age where something traumatic happened (maybe your parents divorced, there was a death or you were bullied at school) and that experience and 'bad feelings' have stuck with you since then.

Do inner child meditation #2 and as you call forth your inner child, specifically give her what she most wanted at that time (reassurance, love, words of appreciation, physical touch in the form of hugs). Don't hold back, this is how you are going to re-parent your inner child and stop her from being needy and causing self-sabotage and other emotional temper tantrums in your adult life.

Playwork: Do inner child meditation #2
You can find the Playwork here:
www.norawendel.com/confidentsexyfree

Journal after doing inner child meditation #2; journalling is a beautiful way to get out of your head and release stored emotions and feelings that aren't serving you.

And breathe.

These two meditations on loving up my inner child were such a big healing in my need for validation and love. I celebrate you and am so proud of you for doing this here with me.

It doesn't stop there. You can integrate inner child loving into your everyday life. I talk to my inner child daily. *I tell her how much I love her, how proud I am of her, how I am always here for her, that she can tell me anything, that we get to be best friends, that I will never leave her.*

Just writing this brings such softness to my being because I mean it. I will never leave myself, it's my promise to myself. My little Nora wants to hear that every day. She wants to be seen, heard and appreciated and I give it to her daily so she doesn't have to throw her emotional temper tantrums anymore. I suggest you do the same. Love her up on the daily and just feel how it softens up your self-love.

Understanding Your Core Wounds

Your core wound is the one biggest story you tell yourself every single day (based on a childhood internalised unmet emotional need) that rules your adult life. We have many stories and beliefs yet there is always ONE (sometimes two) that are on repeat, whether we realise it or not.

Mine is: *I am not worthy of being loved.*

And it stemmed from me 'thinking' I had to prove myself to get my dad's love—totally not true, and yet I believed that. It shows up in my life as feeling not worthy to get new clients or as feeling like I need to prove how awesome I am in my love relationships ...

This is also when I notice my self-sabotage pop up; I'm highly aware of me wanting to be validated with love so I can feel my worth. In a relationship I can see when I'm 'trying' to be ultra-loving and doting so I can get the love back. I then stop and catch myself. I talk to my inner child and tell her how much I love her and how she doesn't need the love from anyone else.

By knowing you inner child's unmet emotional needs, you can catch yourself as an adult playing out that emotional temper tantrum and then with the awareness, take a step back, calmly talk to your inner child, send her love, and tell her you can handle this situation, take a breath, and then take action as is needed, as a calm and collected adult. The opposite would be a quick emotional reaction stemming from that unstable, needy, emotional child.

Catching yourself out like this feels like serious adulting; it takes practice, and the more you do it the easier it gets. Here are the journalling questions to become aware of and catch yourself playing out your biggest core wound (aka lie) about yourself.

journalling questions

What is my biggest core wound?

How is it affecting my life?

How would my life be different if I didn't believe that?

What came up? Have you ever thought about this before? I didn't and when I did this exercise and saw how I felt unworthy to be loved, I also saw how silly it was!

Let's move on to understanding how to stop the self-sabotage and yes, it has to do with your inner child.

Understanding Self-Sabotage

Self-sabotage is a behaviour or action that you do (consciously or unconsciously) that interferes with you achieving your desires or goals.

Let me tell you, we all self-sabotage, no need to feel shameful or guilty. Self-sabotage can look any number of ways: from procrastination, to overeating, to numbing yourself out, to not doing your finances, to always wearing the same clothes.

Self-sabotage is linked to your beliefs and stories of who you think you can or cannot be. It's these underlying beliefs (which we uncovered in Chapter 1) that give the fuel to your self-sabotage, and where do the beliefs come from? You guessed it, the theme of this chapter: childhood.

It's time to get clear on your own sabotaging patterns by journalling on them. Again, this isn't a single-use journalling question. Our sabotages can change according to our desires or goals and change as we grow too!

journalling question

What are my obvious self-sabotaging patterns?

Self-sabotage isn't bad, it's simply the brain thinking it's not safe to proceed forward, so all panic buttons get hit and you retreat back into what you know as comfortable or good. I like to have fun with myself when I recognise my self-sabotage. Here's how I do it: I catch myself out, I look at what my underlying fear or belief may be that is causing me to sabotage, I tell myself that it is safe to proceed while loving up my inner child, and then I make a commitment to move forward anyway, all with self-compassion and kindness.

Here's my formula:

Four-Step Self-Sabotage Stopper

1. **Catch your self-sabotage**
2. **Tell yourself you are safe and can move forward whilst loving your inner child**
3. **Look at an underlying belief or fear that may be causing the sabotage**
4. **Move forward with kindness and compassion towards yourself**

Use this formula whenever you feel stuck, frustrated and not moving forward when you know you should totally be rocking your goals. Listen, love, nothing is going to work if you don't do the (play)work. Think of it as fun; you are so much more likely to do fun things than 'work' things, right? Hence, all the inner work is called playwork in my book.

Grateful for where I'm at.
Excited about where I'm going.

You Got You

Inner children, core wounds and self-sabotage make up a huge part of who we are and how we show up or don't show up. From reading this chapter you can see how giving attention to your inner child allows her to feel the validation she so craved, freeing her up from causing disruptive patterns of behaviour in your adult life. Similarly, understanding your core wound allows you to empower yourself and not fall into self-deprecating behaviours and instead act from a place of 'I got this'. Knowing how you are sabotaging your own success will only lead you to be even more successful.

Big love!

We covered the groundwork of why we are believing and acting the way we do. "Onwards," as Elizabeth Gilbert always says; there is more fun to be had in becoming that confident, sexy and wildly free version of you. In the next chapter I'm going to be breaking down why I dislike the term self-love and how you go from feeling self-hate to *loving yourself up in all the ways*.

And if I asked you to name all the things you love, how long would it take for you to name yourself?

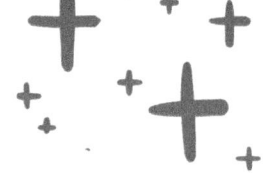

chapter 3
loving yourself

This chapter is all about learning to love yourself, from loving who you are right now, to who you were up until this moment. Self forgiveness plays a big part here.

I'm going to start this chapter with a bold claim that the foundational NEED of all humans is to feel loved. We are constantly seeking love from the moment we are born to the moment we die. It is the underlying current of human existence.

Who is the man I will marry (to feel loved) ...
What is my tribe going to be like (so I can feel loved) ...
Clothes, behaviour, actions, FB posts, it all leads to wanting to feel loved.

Your soul is crying out, *"Am I loved? Somebody, please love me!"*

This soul yearning for love feels even more potent when you weren't given the love you a) deserved and b) longed for as a child. You saw this clearly in Chapter 2.

Understanding that you want to be loved will show you how you are messing up getting that love in your life

right now. Look at your life and see how the theme of wanting love is showing up in your life.

Here are some examples to get you thinking:

Neediness? Wanting to be loved.
Brashness? Wanting to be loved.
People pleasing? Wanting to be loved.
Fear of rejection? Wanting to be loved.
Abandonment issues? Wanting to be loved.
Can't share your voice? Wanting to be loved.

Everything we do is because deep down we want to be loved. We think we have to be different, *'like her'* to be loved—skinnier, fatter, longer hair, make more money, have the man with the business... Those aren't empowering thoughts; you get to decide that you are lovable. If you had some experiences in your childhood that made you internalise you weren't lovable, it's probably still there right now and showing up as:

That client didn't sign on to my program; I'm not lovable.
That man didn't return my text; I'm not lovable.
No one is commenting on my post; I'm not lovable.

We really do think like that and can you see how silly it is AND at the same time how valid your feelings are?

Send your inner child some love right now: *"I know you want to be loved, I'll love you!"*

A phrase I started to say to myself over and over again, and I got this from Marissa Peer, is "I am lovable." When I first heard her speak about how the majority of us don't love ourselves or yearn to be loved yet believe we aren't lovable, I felt whole body tingles (my sign of the universe going YES). I immediately starting saying to myself:

"I am lovable.
I am lovable.
I AM LOVABLE.
I am MF lovable.
Of course I am lovable.
I am amazing.
I am so lovable.
I rock.
I attract love into my life.
I AM LOVABLLLLEEEEEE."

Yep, pretty much like that, getting more and more excited over the fact that yes, indeed, I am lovable.

Playwork: Start saying "I am lovable" over and over to yourself every day. Write it on Post-it Notes on your mirror. Stick it on your car steering wheel. Save it as a screensaver on your

phone. Get it into your head that YOU ARE LOVABLE!

Hashtag #confidentsexyfree and share your "I am lovable" post it notes on Instagram to inspire your followers to love themselves too.

That feels like I went on a bit of a rant there, phew. I'm highly passionate about this because believing you are lovable is the same as believing you are worthy.

Now that I have got you into a state of excitement at the possibility of being lovable and welcoming more love into your life, I want to look at how your need for love is being met in either a healthy or unhealthy way. It's time to whip out your journal and put pen to paper.

journalling questions

How is my need for love showing up in my life?

What are my patterns around getting love?

How do I feel loved?

Some examples: *You may be constantly seeking validation through your posts on Facebook. The energy behind them is look at me, validate me, tell me how amazing I am because I can't see that for myself.*

Or

You may be a chronic people pleaser, saying yes to clients that you know won't work for you, not being able to hold your boundaries around your family and saying yes to doing things for friends even though you really don't want to. You say yes because you fear that if you say no, they'll turn on you and hate you or push you out of their lives.

Your turn to take a look at how the need to be loved is making you behave in ways that you actually don't want to. Think back to that question in Chapter 1: who do you want to be? Reflect if that confident, sexy and wildly free version of yourself acts out of neediness in terms of love.

You may have recognised some silly love self-sabotage patterns through the above journalling playwork and you are ready to change those and ask, "How?"

How do you go about **knowing** you want love and to **actually feeling** loved?

The answer lies in tuning into your feelings, getting clear on **how you feel loved** and then not being afraid to ask for it!

If you want to know more about learning how you feel loved then I highly recommend the book *The Five Love Languages* by Gary Chapman; you can even do a quiz on his website. According to Chapman there are five primary love languages, the way that you understand love: physical touch, acts of service, quality time, gifts and affirmations. We generally have two love languages that when someone does this towards us we **FEEL** the love. Mine are gifts and affirmations, it's also the two that I give out the most to others (a clue to what yours might be, what do you do for others all the time? If you want more clarity do the quiz!).

I very clearly can see in my life when I feel lacking in love—I feel lonely, I feel like none of my friends want to hang out with me, I feel small and shy when I go out to social events. That's not me! I then ask myself what I need; maybe it's a message from a friend (gifts, meaning that idea that someone thought of me is my top love language), or maybe it's asking a friend to directly tell me how much they appreciate me in their life. I ask for what I need in terms of feeling appreciated and loved and therefore my need gets satisfied and I don't have to act in manipulative ways (self-manipulative too!).

These questions will start to get you thinking about the role that love plays in your life. Love is the foundation of life so having a clear idea of a) where you feel lacking in love b) what childhood experience had you feeling that way (this was Chapter 2 work) c) how the neediness for love is showing up in your life and d) giving yourself permission to ask for your love needs will all empower you to show up for yourself more in life.

I had to share all this about love first before I talk about self-love, as lack of self-love is in itself just you trying to get love (by a dark and twisted way of punishing yourself).

be patient
with
yourself.

Loving Yourself Up Aka
Self-~~Love~~-Appreciation

What is self-love? It's such a big term that's casually thrown around online these days and it makes me roll my eyes. My clients always tell me, "I get the whole *idea* of self-love, and yet I don't feel it. *HOW* do I start to feel it?"

That's what this part of the book is about: learning to embody that feeling of *"Wow, I love ME so much, more of ME please!"*

I personally don't resonate with the term self-love, I prefer to use the term *self-appreciation*. It feels more digestible and hints to HOW you can bring that embodied feeling of loving yourself into your life. The word itself, *appreciate*, means to rise up, to increase. When I talk about self-appreciation I'm talking about appreciating (giving gratitude) to who I am and what I do, no matter what. That's the important bit, appreciating every bit of me, the me that is right here, right now.

During my chronic anxiety days I was deeply intertwined in loathing myself for having anxiety and for not being 'normal' (with 'normal' being those confident, sexy and free women I saw everywhere). The self-hating felt like I was constantly picking at a festering wound, causing me more pain and yet I couldn't stop myself from picking at it.

It's a touchy topic because so many women go through self-hate which is nothing more than an underlying lack of self-worth. Self-hate can be compared to an inner bully; no matter what you do, you constantly criticise yourself, put yourself down and feel shitty about who you are.

I used to bully myself for not looking like I wanted to look. I used to bully myself for not being smarter. I used to bully myself for not feeling secure about money. I used to bully myself for not going to yoga more. I could add to my list of 'faults' daily.

I'm not going to ask you to list your 'faults' as I am sure you can spin them off right away without needing a journalling question. I will, however, teach you how to turn the self-hate into self-compassion.

Let me tell you a story. I was living in New Delhi, India when I had my second bout of severe anxiety around four to five years after my first panic attack in London. I decided to leave New Delhi and fly to Goa (further south in India) to be around my dad for a few months and of course be supported in my mini life crisis. It was there I did some counselling with a beautiful woman named Akash Dharmaraj (sending her so much love as she passed onwards this year). We were ending our current pre-paid sessions and I wanted to continue working with her; the thing was, I didn't feel confident enough going to the ATM to withdraw money that I needed to pay her with. I felt stuck; I remember crying with such fear that I would have to go to the ATM alone on my scooter and that I would feel so anxious that I would bring on another panic attack. Akash looked at me and asked me why I didn't ask for help to go to the ATM. "What do you mean?" I asked back. "Why don't you ask your taxi driver to come to the ATM with you?" she said. "I can't do that", I thought to myself, "what would he think?" I struggled back and forth in my head whilst Akash just watched me. "You can do it," she said to me after seeing my internal conflict battle it out in my head.

The next day I asked my taxi driver to come with me to the ATM which was located inside the bank about a 20-minute drive away from where I was staying. Of course he didn't mind, he was getting paid to do it! I got the cash out and handed it to Akash the next session we had. I felt so proud. I did it! I always remember this as a lesson that I can ask for help, I don't need to stay in my own suffering silence as I was often doing during my big bouts of anxiety. I didn't have to be so hard on myself.

Another lesson Akash taught me was self-compassion. I had a hard time leaving my 'safety' comfort zone without feeling anxious and panicky. She told me to just take one step outside my house, then return if I felt too uncomfortable, praising myself that I actually went outside! The next day I could walk down the street a little further before returning to the safety of my home. Again praising my progress (instead of berating myself for not doing more).

I used this self-compassion technique when I lived in Cape Town with my then partner; this was about six months after getting counselling with Akash. I still had anxiety. It was a new city, a new country where on top of my low level anxiety (which was totally linked to lack of self-worth and purpose), crime was at forefront of everyone's mind as this was South Africa. We were living in an apartment in the good area of town and I wanted to go to the coffee shop down the street to do some work (I was a graphic/website designer in those days). I was tormented inside; I felt anxious, I couldn't go, fear was stopping me, yet I was dying to get outside. The internal conflict was eating at me. I packed my bags and left the apartment, went to the gate and freaked out and went back inside. The negative self-talk spiralled out of control and I felt so miserable until my partner came home.

The next day I had the same feelings of frustration. This time I managed to get halfway down the street before freaking out. Back inside the apartment I decided to be kinder to myself, telling myself, "Look how far you got, well done! We can try again tomorrow." The next day I managed to get to the cafe, sit down, order, then freak out and leave. Day by day over a few weeks I finally managed to sit at that cafe and not run away with the anxiety tearing at me. I was so proud of myself!

If I would have allowed my negative self-talk to continue I would have ended up a sobbing mess. That wouldn't have gotten me to the cafe at all. I had the self-compassion to keep trying (I wanted to get out of that apartment so bad!) until I reached my goal.

I've kept this high level of self-compassion from then on. I know the power self-compassion gives to feeling worthy. It's like a mini pep talk: *"You got this, you are amazing, you can do anything, don't worry, if it doesn't work now, it will work later, you rock, you're rocking your life, look at you go ..."*

I want you to start talking to yourself like this. You can copy these words down in your journal and read them out loud to yourself every morning and every night.

Playwork: Start talking to yourself like your own best friend, encouraging and empowering

If you want some inspiration on what to say you can download the PDF for self-compassion from the resource library online. [www.norawendel.com/confidentsexyfree]

be such
a beautiful soul
that people crave
your vibes

Remember, a magnetic woman is a woman who is empowered and empowers others. She doesn't talk herself down all the time. Be careful of how you talk to yourself. It matters.

To make sure you really understand what self-love is when you hear others talk about it I want you to include all the terms below in your definition of self-love:

Self-appreciation
Self-compassion
Self-kindness
Self-care
Self-attention

Self-love is you being your own best friend. It's you being kind to yourself, no matter what. Journal on these questions below to understand how you can change the behaviour towards yourself into more open-hearted loving.

journalling questions

How can I be kinder to myself?

What can I start saying to myself with compassion?

Self-love is really about lathering yourself up in love and stopping the inner bully. A great way to stop the inner bully is to write down what you appreciate about yourself. I do this daily. As a playwork I'm going to get you to double down and write down 50, yes 50!, things you appreciate about yourself.

They don't all have to be huge things; they can be like "I appreciate my body for keeping me alive" or "I appreciate the way I can talk about my feelings so openly." You can also include the little things (you can include whatever you appreciate about yourself!) such as "I appreciate my smile" or "I appreciate the time I give myself to journal every day" or "I appreciate I got out of bed this morning."

Fifty things, love, challenge yourself!

journalling question

What are 50 things you appreciate about yourself? Finish this sentence in your journal: "I appreciate _____ about myself" or "I appreciate that I _____"

If you want to continue this self-appreciation practice daily, then you can write down three things you appreciate about yourself every morning/evening.

I consider this different to gratitude as more often than not when we practise gratitude it's external and outward. We don't often include ourselves. However, when I say appreciate yourself, it's all about you and how awesome you truly are! Yes, even the little things you do are awesome.

~

Self-appreciation isn't the only practice I do to cultivate more 'I am awesome!' vibes. I also practise self-forgiveness and EFT tapping. You may be reading this and still don't feel a shift in your self-hate; that's okay, it takes practice, it's an art. Keep up the positive self-talk, use my PDF as a script and just read off it. Try the 50 things self-appreciation playwork as well as these next two practices. You got this! I believe in you.

Self-forgiveness is just like the forgiveness we did for our parents (or primary caretakers) in Chapter 2; this time it's just directed back at you.

Playwork: Write a list of all the regrets or mistakes you think you have made in your life. It's time to forgive yourself for them!

Once you have your list, simply read out the Ho'oponopono forgiveness mantra: *I'm sorry, please forgive me, I thank you, I love you.*

Then cross off that incident on your list and from your life! Sometimes you have to do it more than once; that's okay too!

Remember when you wanted what you currently have?

B *I* U̲ 📎   **Send to Self**

The whole idea is to cultivate that internal muscle of self-compassion. Those mistakes you made (or think they were mistakes) were probably because you wanted to keep yourself safe and protected at that time (remember the brain functions from Chapter 1?). There are never mistakes or failures, just opportunities to continuously navigate towards how you want to feel; more on that in Chapter 5.

Want to feel even more self-compassion? Do Ho'oponopono forgiveness whilst doing EFT tapping. When I do this I feel the intensity of the compassion increase and at the end of the tapping I feel GREAT and feeling great is how I want to live my life, don't you?

EFT stands for Emotional Freedom Technique (also called tapping) and it's a healing tool that works by tapping on certain meridian points on the body to release blocked energy and emotions. I first used it just after my panic attack in London and it helped me get back onto the buses in London (imagine walking everywhere, it took ages and was impractical in winter with loads of bags).

I made you a selection of tapping videos that you can follow along. Do the tapping for self-forgiveness first. I want you to notice the shift in your energy as you do the tapping. You can download the video and keep it on your phone for easy access.

Playwork: Do the EFT tapping video for self-forgiveness
Find the video here: www.norawendel.com/confidentsexyfree

Doing EFT is one of my favourite ways to shift energy quickly (along with NLP). I tap daily on whatever issue I have in my life. I always notice myself feeling better after a session of tapping. I don't do it at home exclusively; I tap on my beach walk, I tap when I sit in a cafe, I tap in aeroplanes.

Tap tap tap.
Forgive forgive forgive.

You can always be kinder to yourself, you can always forgive yourself, you can always find more ways to love yourself up. Catch your negative Nancy giving you a speech and butter her up as well! Make the choice right now to only talk beautiful, opening, expansive things about yourself. It works.

Learning to be kind to yourself is a big part of owning your worth. You can't believe you are the 'hot shit' (with the biggest heart) and not actually love who you are deep down. That deep self-appreciation is what oozes radiance in women; it makes men attracted to you for when you love yourself you are sending out the vibrations of love. Love attracts more love and isn't love what we truly desire?

~

I'm checking in with you, how are you feeling? Are things shifting within you? We've unravelled a whole bunch of deep stuff already in Chapters 1 – 3. From limiting beliefs, to how your inner child just wants to be appreciated, to learning how to start accepting more of who you are through self-appreciation and self-forgiveness.

If you have any questions you can always send me a DM on Instagram with a voice note or video. You can find me here: @norawendel

Oh, I can't wait to share with you more about welcoming in your womanhood in Chapter 4 because if you want to be a confident, sexy and wildly free woman, you have to understand what being a woman means and how femininity plays such a big role in calling that ease, grace and flow into your life.

FEMME
FIERCE
FIGHTER

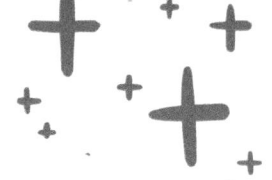

chapter 4
womanhood

I can't write a book about how to turn into a confident, sexy and free woman without sharing my journey about reconnecting to my femininity and ultimately my womanhood. I'll start with a little backstory as to why I ended up so disconnected from my sensuality, sexuality and femininity.

I grew up in Nepal and went to an amazing international boarding school in India (look up United World Colleges) for my formative teenage years (16 − 18). I was carefree, wild with my joy and totally open. I remember during my first year at boarding something inside me shifted where I didn't feel safe to be so open and carefree anymore. I didn't have ONE big traumatic experience, it was more like a few smaller incidents that left me feeling uneasy. I started to cover up more, I started to not be so wildly open with my attitude.

I remember one incident where there were 15 of us teenagers piled into the local town Jeep, squished in with another 10 local people all wanting to go into the big city of Pune. We were piled in tight (more money for the transport guys) so people were hanging off the side of the non-existent doors and hanging off the back

bumper; it was the norm, it was India, after all. I was sitting in the front next to the driver, the front being the most comfortable, in my opinion. My legs were right beside the stick shift. For 45 bumpy minutes I was so aware that the driver (a man) was brushing my leg every time he shifted gears. It was uncomfortable and I think it was from then on I decided that I had to be more careful with being myself (a woman in India).

Like I mentioned, it wasn't a traumatic experience, it just left a 'feel bad' memory in my brain which then caused me to believe that I wasn't safe being a fully expressed woman. Having my panic attack and the after-effect of chronic anxiety didn't help my self-expression either. I wasn't comfortable with my own body, always fearing it would betray me again. It wasn't until I moved to Ubud, Bali that I saw how disconnected from myself, my sensuality, my sexuality and my womanhood I had become.

It was time to find myself again. Ubud was the perfect place to explore movement, dance, singing, tantra and authentic relating, all bringing me back to trust myself, my body and feel the aliveness of life and the beauty of being a woman. This is what we are going to be diving into right now.

~

What is your relationship to yourself? Do you honour your body, track your menstrual cycle, find self-expression through movement, art or writing? Or are you the kind of go go go woman, feeling edgy and hard, not stopping for self-appreciation?

I see more and more women today following the masculine way of life—striving for goals, never satiated, actively pushing forward, never giving space for rest, always on the go for more more and more. This isn't the feminine way.

The feminine way is one of ease, of joy, of receiving, of feeling, of playing, of being sensually ALIVE.

Society progresses by moving forward constantly, it needs the masculine energy of competition and of hard edginess in order to thrive and since we are brought up with society as our external influence and many of us internalise the same tendencies without ever questioning it.

I'm not against the masculine way, we need it in our lives as much as we need the ease and grace of femininity. What I see, however, is that women have lost touch with the art of being a woman. I know because it happened to me. If you want to be a confident, sexy and wildly free woman you have to **own** the fact that you are a woman; this owning is what cultivates that magnetism I talk about.

I'm going to put my disclaimer here: I'm not against men and I don't want to exclude transgender, non-binary or any other beautiful people who choose how they want to be in this world, and at the same time I teach femininity to women who are biological women and choose to be identified by that. The work I teach is based off my own experience and I am a CIS woman.

I want to make it clear that when I talk about femininity I'm not talking about wearing flowy dresses, long hair, makeup or the like. I talk about femininity as the energy behind your actions, the softness with which you approach yourself and life, the pleasure you get out of being you, the ease of how you choose to show up knowing you got this, and the strength and resilience of not backing down from your goals. At the same time you can totally wear those feather-light cotton kaftans, wrap flower crowns around your head or wear Louboutin heels and that killer red lippy. You do you.

That woman you can't keep your eyes off who exudes so much confidence, self-worth and personal power, she is in touch with ALL of herself. I call that being *a fully embodied sensual woman.*

What Is a Fully Embodied Sensual Woman?

I define a fully embodied woman as a woman who:
Knows what she wants
Knows her desires
Feels alive with the idea of possibilities
Is tuned in to herself
Feels it all
Is highly sensual
Exudes confidence
Knows her self-worth
Loves pleasure
Is deeply connected to her body
Listens to her intuition
Is fully receptive (not passive) and in flow
Consciously chooses how she wants to feel.

Shivers. Even I read that list and go, "YES, I want that!" Don't you? A fully embodied sensual woman is deeply connected to herself *in all ways.* Ask yourself, out of that list, what do you need to welcome more into your life? That's a great starting place for reconnecting.

I want to differentiate between womanhood and femininity. Womanhood is the nature of being a woman, it's our bodies, our state, our qualities.

Whereas femininity is about the energy and attributes of a woman. For me, they are inextricably intertwined and both owning your womanhood and cultivating your femininity makes for a va-va-voom woman!

journalling question
What do I need to welcome more of in order to become a fully embodied sensual woman?

Welcoming in the Feminine

Learning how to cultivate the feminine in a healthy way will lead to that deeper reconnection to your womanhood and ultimately your power.

Side note: if you don't think women are powerful consider the fact that a) we create life b) there is nothing more alluring than a woman who wants something and goes for it and c) the fierceness and strength that a woman will embody when there is a threat to her children is an uncontained force.

Power. Women are pure power. You, my love, are powerful.

Okay, back to the feminine. The feminine is about receiving, allowing, nurturing, creating beauty, cultivating empathy, intuition and learning how to feel deeply.

Being in your feminine feels like the following:

- Joy
- Relief
- Peacefulness
- Calmness
- Groundedness
- Aliveness
- Juiciness
- Softness
- Strength
- Beauty
- Playfulness
- Emotional maturity

Out of this list, what do you feel like you want more of in your life right now? Pen to paper, love!

journalling question

How can I tune into more of my femininity?

You can go down that list above and ask yourself, how can I welcome more joy into my life? What brings me joy? How can

I be more grounded? How can I create more beauty around me and so forth ...

I like to notice what I feel like I am missing (by doing the journalling above) and then making an intention to simply allow more of that into my life. Remember that YOU get to decide what makes you feel joyful/ beautiful/playful, etc. It's based on the FEELING. For example, I may get my nails done to feel more feminine and beautiful, I may put on a face mask or buy myself flowers to add beauty to my home.

I'm excited for your uncovering!

Apart from journalling there are also other ways to cultivate more femininity. If you really feel dry, rough, anxiety-ridden, doubting, try these next few reconnection tools which I personally use.

How to Cultivate Your Femininity

How do you cultivate your femininity? By feeling, by moving, by allowing your sensuality to blossom, by taking yourself less seriously. Here's what I did to tune inwards and nurture my inner flower.

1. Feeling

Women are natural feelers; our positive poles of energy are at our hearts, our heart is our feeling centre. Remember that everything we want in life is to feel a certain way (Chapter 1). Becoming so highly attuned to your feelings allows you to navigate away from what doesn't work for you and makes you feel bad to what does work for you and makes you feel great.

Let yourself feel through your heart, don't close down that portal of femininity (which we often do when we get hurt).

With feelings it is important to remember to simply embrace them, ride the wave and then let them go. Often we like to create stories that turn into mini reality TV series full of drama. Don't allow your feelings to take over your life. Always allow them to be there then let them fade. Neuroscience has shown that an emotion lasts for 90 seconds, only 90 seconds; the rest is us creating a story around it. Go and read Joan Rosenberg's book *90 Seconds to a Life You Love*; she talks all about this.

Feel it, embrace it, ride it, let it go.

And remember that your feelings are always valid.

Playwork: Close your eyes and tune into what you are feeling right now. Notice, embrace and let it go. You can do this multiple times a day to start tuning your feeling radar

2. Moving

Women vibrate with the energy of creation; we create life! In Hinduism women are known to be called Shakti, a term that denotes the pure vibration that creates life. It is the union of Shakti with Shiva (Shiva being the masculine, ever-pervasive, still consciousness) that created life as we know it. Women are born to move.

What kind of movement? Any movement that you feel in tune with. Dancing, walking, shaking ... allow the energy of life to flow through you. What happens when you don't move? Stagnation, like the dirty pool of water trapped between rocks in a river, it goes murky and who knows what decides to live in that murky cesspit. Stagnation in women creates dullness, dryness and lifelessness.

Want to feel alive, vibrant and radiant? Move your body in whatever way you feel called to (trust your intuition).

If you close your eyes and tune into the aliveness of your body, you can hear your body screaming "I am ALIVE" pulsing through every one of your cells.

Playwork: Move that body of yours. Sigh, scream, dance, walk. Allow the energy of life to flow through you, don't hold it in

3. Sensuality

Our senses are how we interpret reality. It's the filter through which we form our thoughts. Our senses also allow us to experience pleasure (and pain). I use sensuality as a way to reconnect myself to the beauty of being alive. I define sensuality as an enriching of our life experience precisely because if we concentrate on heightening the awareness of our senses we start to feel more!

How can you attune yourself more to your senses? By slowing down, becoming mindful of each experience. Slow eating, slow lovemaking, slow self-pleasure. It comes down to feeling more and more. Use essential oils, massage your own body. Eat delicious chocolate and savour it piece by piece. Listen to sensual music.

Playwork: Close your eyes—tune into your senses. What does the air feel like on your skin right now? What is the furthest sound you can hear? How is the light reflecting off your closed eyelids?

It is because we live in a masculine fast-paced world that we often forget to tune inwards to listen and to feel. Women often come up to me and tell me how vibrant I am; it's because I allow myself to tune into the aliveness of everything around me. I tune into the feeling of joy, of beauty, of YES, I GET TO BE HERE!

I created a meditation for you, it's similar to the same process I use in my own meditation to drop deep into the feeling of "I get to be here, I get to feel all this, I get to be alive." I do a form of this meditation daily.

Playwork: Listen to the joy of being alive meditation to feel how you can tune yourself (daily) into choosing to feel great

Find the meditation here: www.norawendel.com/confidentsexyfree

SUNSHINE STATE OF MIND

Music also helps to heighten feelings. I created a playlist on Spotify called Sensual Sundays which are my favourite songs to drop me deep into my sensuality.

Sensuality tip: I often found myself clenching my jaw when dancing, doing hard tasks or worrying. I now consciously relax my jaw, allowing my mouth to open and then sighing with a big exhalation. I find this allows my parasympathetic nervous system to feel safe and relax even more. The parasympathetic nervous system is responsible for our rest and digest activities, the feel-good activities (instead of the flight, fight or stress). Sigh, sigh, sigh and sigh some more.

Playwork: Listen to my Sensual Sunday playlist and drop into a state of feeling. Feel your body, your skin, feel the music and how you want to move to it. There is no wrong way to feel

Find the Sensual Sunday playlist here: www.norawendel.com/confidentsexyfree

4. Create Beauty

I love creating beauty! I just can't help myself. Creating beauty doesn't just mean dolling yourself up (I do that too though); it can be anything from buying and arranging flowers in your house, repainting your office, adorning yourself with jewellery or tattoos... Creating beauty softens the heart.

Create beauty for the sake of beauty, not for validation or for people pleasing. Beauty is whatever *feels* beautiful for you! It may even be rearranging the apps on your phone into colour-coordinated folders, and yes, I have several friends who love doing that.

When you feel beautiful it leads to more confidence. Wearing granny panties and old joggers to the shop around the corner may be practical yet you probably don't feel beautiful in it. When I feel low self-worth and confidence I make sure I up my beauty regimes. I buy flowers, I wear my 'feel great' clothes, I get my nails done. All of this I do for me, so that I can feel beautiful, not for anyone else. Everyone else gets to feel the effects though!

Playwork: How can you create more beauty in your life starting right now?

Maybe it's clearing up a mess you made in one of your rooms, maybe it is buying flowers or wearing your favourite dress. Make a list of things you can do to cultivate more beauty in your life right now.

5. Play

We take this adulting so seriously. Playfulness is a big part of the feminine. It's also highly attractive! No one likes to hang around someone who takes themselves so seriously, can't laugh and doesn't like to have fun.

Laugh and be silly. Playing with kids is a great way to welcome in more playfulness as they have no end to ideas and silly games to play. If you have perfectionistic tendencies, go play with kids and they'll show you how to just let go and be in the moment, messy or not.

Go to a comedy show for some laughs. Stop taking your life so seriously. We want to live life in order to feel great and playing helps with that. When you can adopt a playful attitude towards creating the life you desire, it just becomes more fun, more adventurous, less of a 'task'. Think back to when you last had fun and played, didn't time just go by? Didn't you forget all your worries? Didn't you activate a flow state where you just got to be you without any of your limiting beliefs? Yep. Playtime is awesome.

Playwork: Go have some fun, schedule it in. Ask yourself, what do I like to do to have fun in my life?

~

Tuning into feeling more, moving your body to avoid stagnancy, dropping into the richness of your senses, dedicating yourself to creating beauty and becoming more playful are all ways that I allowed more of the feminine energy into my life. I started to soften, I felt free within my heart, life became pleasurable, I felt alive and vibrant.

Is there such a thing as over cultivation of feminine energy? Yep! I see it in some women, showing up particularly strong around the conscious community. Women always say things like "I'm going with the flow" and then never take personal responsibility or think that someone or the universe will do 'everything' for them; nope, inspired action is needed too to make things happen. Too much feminine energy is called toxic femininity.

HAVE YOU LOVED YOU TODAY?

X

The Role of Toxic Femininity

Toxic femininity is:

Self-doubt
Self-hate
Gossiping
Lack of structure and being disorganised
Manipulative tendencies
Jealousy
Being overly emotional
Taking everything personally
Constant approval seeking
Lack of personal responsibility

All of these point towards a lack of self-worth ultimately. Watch out for these tendencies in your own life. You can avoid tipping over into toxic femininity by simply being aware *what* toxic femininity is and catching yourself out when you start acting in that way. No need for that.

Notice when you are tipping the scale over into any of the above ways of being. Ask yourself, "Is this what my confident, sexy and free self would do?" (highly unlikely). Know your boundaries, ride your emotions to then let them go, understand comparison, judgment and jealousy is your inner child acting up with her unmet emotional needs. That's how you become a deeply connected woman, and you are already blossoming into her.

Definitely my favourite part of welcoming in my femininity, aka the power I have as a woman, is aligning myself with the idea that my life gets to be easy, in flow and full of grace.

Ease, Flow and Grace

During my anxiety days I *struggled*. I struggled with myself, my worth, my doubt and taking action. Life didn't seem easy. I internalised beliefs that getting things done was hard, that making money meant I had to work hard, that getting clients was hard, that I could never be 'successful'.

As I grow further and further into my personal development journey I know that I can be a conscious creatress of my own life (how empowering is that?!). As a Human we have the distinct ability to CHOOSE how we want to think and therefore how we want to feel. Doing the same belief work as in Chapter 1, I saw that my belief about life being hard was stopping me. I decided to change my belief.

What if you just decided life could be easy?

That's what I did. I didn't want my life to be a struggle, I'd been through that. I wanted the universe to *always* be on my side. I could choose to think that and feel into that ease; that felt good, that felt great!

Ask yourself ...

journalling question

How would my life change if I
decided life could be easy?

How would that change your beliefs, your actions and
then your reality if you decided life could be easy and
the universe was always on your side?

Feel good belief: Life gets to be easy.

Ease is definitely the way of the feminine; you know
what else is? Flow and grace. I journal on this most
weeks because I know (from past experience) that I
make my life harder than it has to be, often thinking I
have to do it all alone, that I'm not supported, that I'm
lacking in some way (lies, lies, lies!).

journalling question

How can I have more ease, grace
and flow in my life?

Call in that ease, flow and grace into your life right now. It feels so freeing, so much more in alignment when you decide that your life can be that way. This also includes your internal struggles, okay? You get to choose. Struggle and frustration or ease and flow? I know which ones I want!

Feel good belief: I love feeling ease, grace and flow in my life.

I'm going to end this chapter on womanhood and femininity touching on the menstrual cycle, a beautiful and unique aspect of being a woman. I'm only going to touch on this topic here as this can be a whole book in itself (go google, some great books out there!). I cover this topic in more depth in some of my online programs. Check out my website for more info.

If you don't track your cycle I suggest you start. Now you might be on birth control; I was on the pill for many years before switching to the Mirena IUD and then not having a period for three years. I took it out after three years as I felt the hormones in the Mirena were adding to my anxiety and I had candida for five years which made me feel dirty and shameful around sex. The choice is ultimately yours and all I want to add is tune in and ask your body what she wants.

Your body knows, it always has all the answers.

If you do have your menstruation and aren't currently tracking it, I use a (paid) app called Flo. Super easy to input my dates and keep track of feelings/emotions and see if I'm syncing with the new moon!

I used to be one of those women who thought my menstruation was a hindrance not an advantage! How wrong I was.

Through our menstruation cycle women go through rebirth every month. Our bodies are flushed with hormones that are aimed at growing life. During ovulation is the time you'll feel most alive and perky, radiating confidence; it's your body's way of attracting your mate as your egg wants to get fertilised. Once you become aware of this, you'll feel such a big difference, it's amazing. I use this to my advantage! I launch programs during ovulation, I go onto podcasts, I go out more and it feels great.

During menstruation most of us feel smaller, wanting to hibernate and take care of ourselves. I tend to calm down in my business during menstruation. I am not as social and I love to journal, dream and manifest during my menstruation as it's such a great time for self-reflection.

Understanding where you are in your cycle helps in understanding your emotions too! I know I get sensitive and teary eyes a few days before my period. I used to take things so personally during that time, now I just know it's my hormones making me feel that way. No need to allow my inner bully to tell me I am not loved!

Another empowering reason I like to track my cycle is because I use it to my advantage in my business. I do business the feminine way—with ease, flow and grace, of course! Why would I want to push myself and be an extrovert during my menstruation when my body wants to be inside, alone and taking care of itself? I try to organise my launch schedule to coincide when I'm ovulating for maximum sexiness and va-va-voom attractive energy.

Playwork: Start tracking your cycle from now on

See what you notice in terms of your emotions and where you are at in your cycle. You can take this further like I do and start to plan your life and business around your menstruation.

You can't be a fully embodied woman if you don't at least welcome the very part of you that creates life. If you feel very disconnected from everything 'down there' (and maybe you have had some childhood trauma bringing up shame or fear, and that's okay), I have a beautiful meditation that I want you to do that reconnects you back to your womb. The power place of creation. The power of being a woman.

Playwork: Listen to the connect to womb meditation. Afterwards journal on what came up for you

Find the meditation here: www.norawendel. com/confidentsexyfree

~

To become a Queen,
You have to give up
Playing the princess.

-E. Peterson

This chapter has really been about reconnecting to yourself as a woman and allowing more of the ease of femininity to be cultivated in your life. If you don't have a strong connection to yourself, how can you expect anyone else to be able to connect to who you are? This is what self-awareness is.

Knowing what you want. Knowing what triggers you. Knowing what makes you feel great.

No one can give you what you want if you don't know what you like! That's like the waiter asking for your order and you saying, "I don't know, serve me anything," then getting a meal the waiter loves and you can't even take a bite of it.

That simply won't do.

Connect back to yourself and the amazingness of being a woman. You are sexy, you are radiant, you are intuitive, you are playful, you are beautiful, you are a queen.

And what do queens do? They rule their empires with love, devotion and pleasure. Chapter 5 is all about learning what you like, and more specifically, what turns you on. Let's turn on your turn-on.

great things are fucking coming great things are fucking coming great things are fucking coming
great things are fucking coming great things are fucking coming great things are fucking coming
great things are fucking coming great things are fucking coming great things are fucking coming
great things are fucking coming great things are fucking coming great things are fucking coming
great things are fucking coming great things are fucking coming great things are fucking coming
great things are fucking coming great things are fucking coming great things are fucking coming
great things are fucking coming great things are fucking coming great things are fucking coming
great things are fucking coming great things are fucking coming great things are fucking coming
great things are fucking coming great things are fucking coming great things are fucking coming
great things are fucking coming great things are fucking coming great things are fucking coming
great things are fucking coming great things are fucking coming great things are fucking coming
great things are fucking coming great things are fucking coming great things are fucking coming
great things are fucking coming great things are fucking coming great things are fucking coming
great things are fucking coming great things are fucking coming great things are fucking coming
great things are fucking coming great things are fucking coming great things are fucking coming
great things are fucking coming great things are fucking coming great things are fucking coming
great things are fucking coming great things are fucking coming great things are fucking coming
great things are fucking coming great things are fucking coming great things are fucking coming
great things are fucking coming great things are fucking coming great things are fucking coming
great things are fucking coming great things are fucking coming great things are fucking coming
great things are fucking coming great things are fucking coming great things are fucking coming
great things are fucking coming great things are fucking coming great things are fucking coming
great things are fucking coming great things are fucking coming great things are fucking coming
great things are fucking coming great things are fucking coming great things are fucking coming
great things are fucking coming great things are fucking coming great things are fucking coming
great things are fucking coming great things are fucking coming great things are fucking coming
great things are fucking coming great things are fucking coming great things are fucking coming
great things are fucking coming great things are fucking coming great things are fucking coming
great things are fucking coming great things are fucking coming great things are fucking coming
great things are fucking coming great things are fucking coming great things are fucking coming
great things are fucking coming great things are fucking coming great things are fucking coming
great things are fucking coming great things are fucking coming great things are fucking coming
great things are fucking coming great things are fucking coming great things are fucking coming
great things are fucking coming great things are fucking coming **great things are fucking coming**
great things are fucking coming great things are fucking coming great things are fucking coming
great things are fucking coming great things are fucking coming great things are fucking coming
great things are fucking coming great things are fucking coming great things are fucking coming
great things are fucking coming great things are fucking coming great things are fucking coming
great things are fucking coming great things are fucking coming great things are fucking coming
great things are fucking coming great things are fucking coming great things are fucking coming
great things are fucking coming great things are fucking coming great things are fucking coming
great things are fucking coming great things are fucking coming great things are fucking coming
great things are fucking coming great things are fucking coming great things are fucking coming
great things are fucking coming great things are fucking coming great things are fucking coming
great things are fucking coming great things are fucking coming great things are fucking coming
great things are fucking coming great things are fucking coming great things are fucking coming
great things are fucking coming great things are fucking coming great things are fucking coming
great things are fucking coming great things are fucking coming great things are fucking coming
great things are fucking coming great things are fucking coming great things are fucking coming

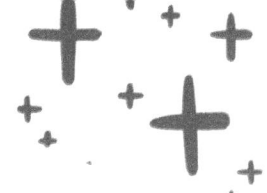

chapter 5
p is for pleasure

Ah, pleasure, pleasure, pleasure. I had such an aversion to even the word pleasure until my thirties. I associated it with sex and for me sex was shameful and therefore I avoided talking and exploring pleasure. Not anymore! Are you ready to explore what pleasure means for you? To understand how to welcome more feel good feelings into your life without feeling guilty? This is what we will unravel in this chapter.

As Humans we are tuned to avoid pain, we do everything to avoid pain. We get our hearts broken and then make silent promises to ourselves to *never* be vulnerable like that again. We navigate life swerving around the mine bombs of pain: "Oops, let's not do that again, that hurt" or "Oh no, it's not safe to express that way, last time it didn't work out for you that well." Pleasure comes second. Isn't that strange?

Why don't we change that around? Let's have pleasure as our driving compass and let the avoidance of pain come second. That's what I changed in my life and my life just gets better and better!

Before I'd stay at home to avoid the pain of my anxiety in unfamiliar situations. I'd not speak up to avoid the pain of rejection in my relationships. I'd make sure I stayed small to avoid the pain of being called out. I lived a life in fear.

Now I ask myself, how can I bring in more pleasure into my life? How can I constantly be moving towards pleasure? What more can I do to open up to pleasure?

The English Oxford Dictionary defines pleasure as:

- a feeling of happy satisfaction and enjoyment
- an event or activity from which one derives enjoyment
- sensual gratification

https://en.oxforddictionaries.com/definition/pleasure

Pleasure is something that makes you feel good. I believe the point of life is *to feel as good as you can in the amount of time we have here.* Why would I want to feel bad? Yet we have this warped idea that we can concentrate on avoiding pain to then feel more pleasure. Instead, let's focus on bringing more pleasure into our lives.

I'm not only talking about sexual pleasure, I'm talking about doing more of the things that make you feel happy, feel joyful, feel grateful, feel expanded, feel good.

Playwork: Make a list of all the things that make you feel good, aka bring you pleasure. Make it a long list of at least 50 things. They can be big like travelling to a new country or small like sipping tea on your balcony in the morning; it all counts if it makes you feel good

Now that you have a list you can start to cultivate a *pleasure practice.* Every day do at least two things from your list; make it a habit to seek out the pleasure in life. This is a daily practice; the more you focus on the small pleasures in life, the more you'll enjoy your life. *Playing this 'game' of pleasure will enhance your experience of life. Life becomes yummy, juicy with fun to be had, feel-good feelings to be felt and good vibes to be spread.*

Your pleasure empowers you.

-Danielle LaPorte

A woman who feels good vibrates the energy of happiness, joy, lightheartedness and that is the energy that makes people want to be around you. No one wants to be hanging out with Debbie Downer, right? You want to be that radiating woman who inspires and empowers; do your pleasure practice every morning and feel the shift.

If you struggle (like I did) to get out of the contracted-fear feelings in your life, I made you a meditation to experience the joy, happiness and lightheartedness that comes with feeling like a radiant woman. It's called radiance meditation. I do a version of this meditation more often than not in the mornings.

Playwork: Do the radiance meditation to really embody what it feels like to be a woman who vibrates positivity and joy. Repeat as often as you desire

Find the radiance meditation here: www.norawendel.com/confidentsexyfree

And how was that experience of the radiance meditation? Did you feel how your energy expanded outwards from your very being and how amazing and empowered you felt? If you wake up feeling low and shitty about yourself, do the radiance meditation, it'll shift your energy.

Using Your Emotions to Guide You to More Pleasure

Who is an Abraham Hicks fan here? (Both my hands shoot up!) If you don't know of them, YouTube is your best buddy; just type in the name and start listening. All I'll say is that they are a channel of higher consciousness that talk a lot about how to feel good about yourself and get anything you want in life. And yes, it all comes down to how you think (Chapter 1 covered this) which influences how you feel.

We live in a world of contrasts, it's the contrast that allows us to feel what we don't like and what we do like; you can call it feel good or feel bad. It's based on these experiences that we can start to formulate how we want to feel in the future—this is exactly what manifestation is, feeling what you want NOW.

For example, you said yes to a work party that you don't want to go to yet feel like you 'should' go to. This is a life situation or an experience. You hate the event, leave feeling grumpy and still have to get up to work the next day. It wasn't a good experience; instead, you would have loved to stay at home, reading in bed with your soft flannel PJs on, drinking a glass of white wine, all snug and comfy. That experience of not upholding your boundary taught you that next time you would rather stay at home.

This is an example of a (seemingly negative) experience showing you what you do want. This is the beauty of being a Human, our ability to choose how we do want to feel. By experiencing the feelings we don't want to feel, we get to know how we do want to feel. We can go about consciously doing those actions or activities that will make us feel good. That's what Abraham calls conscious creating, and when you fully embrace conscious creating life just gets better and better.

This is why I don't believe in negativity in my life, every experience I have which 'feels bad' makes it clearer to me how I do want to feel. Does that make sense to you? I hope it does because this is how I get such clarity towards creating my dream life.

For example, my last long-term relationship ended as we were codependent and it turned emotionally abusive (both our faults). It was because of this experience that I learnt I didn't know how to have nourishing love relationships. This helped me make my decision to study authentic relating, tools and practices I use every day now. I could have easily been heartbroken and pining over him; instead, I had such determination to learn about relationships.

DO LITERALLY WHATEVER MAKES YOU HAPPY

Your turn.

Take some time to do these next journalling questions as when you understand this process of allowing your 'not good feelings' to navigate you towards your 'feel good' feelings you can apply it into your life in every situation. It becomes a constant realignment towards feeling good, aka pleasure.

journalling questions

What is not feeling good in my life right now?

How do I want to feel about that instead?

What can I do to feel that way right now?

Asking myself "How do I want to feel about that instead?" has been my guiding question that has allowed me to shift my lack mindset around money, expanded my online coaching business exponentially and got me out of my constant fear state.

Go on, see if asking yourself that too will change your life just as much as it has mine.

The Story of Not Enoughness or Too Muchness

I am a hedonist, someone who prioritises pleasure in her life. A friend called me that one day and I had to actually google the definition as I became instantly defensive thinking it was all about guilty pleasures. Turns out I totally agreed with him. Yep, that's me. I'm all about pleasure.

Isn't it funny that we associate pleasure with 'too much', like it's a bad thing. Feeling guilty if we partake in it too much, like we have to be struggling in the quagmire of pain. That same conditioning is why women feel like they are too much or too little (I consider it the same).

Lack of self-worth is the feeling of not being enough: good enough, sexy enough, smart enough, you name it.

Our society has intertwined worth with achievement and achievement is nothing more than action. You scroll on Instagram and see that woman who's only 24, has a kid, a thriving business, shows up daily on the platform and you think to yourself, "I'm not enough," I'm not doing all those things like she is which must mean I am not enough.

The conditioning starts in our schooling system with the idea of working hard gets you a gold star (I loved those stars!) which means you get a good grade and also get praised. Praise feels good, it must mean I am loved!

It's the same in our work environments: work good, work hard, get praised and then get a raise.

Can you see why you think your worth is based on your achievements? When I had my anxiety I used to torment myself because I didn't feel like I had a purpose, that I wasn't doing anything with my life. That I wasn't good for anything because of my 'condition'.

If you feel this not 'good enoughness' in your life I want you to journal on the following questions to put into perspective what 'enough' even means for you.

journalling questions

What does 'good enough' even mean?

In relation to whom? To what?

What is enough? What do I have to do to achieve enough?

Enoughness is a concept in our head that often we don't have ANY clarity about; once you can get clearer on your own definition of what enough even is, it's easier to then deconstruct how you can feel enough. Not feeling good enough is a lack of or low self-worth. Remember that low self-worth is a story or belief you allow to run your life that may have been caused by a childhood experience where all you wanted was to be loved and recognised and instead got scolded, hit or just told to go away. That's why the inner child integration playwork is so important in cultivating the feelings of self-worth.

Feeling 'Too Much'

Now what about if you feel like you are 'too much' and you constantly feel like you have to tame yourself down. That is also lack of self-worth. I always tell my clients that nature never tells itself it is too much, it just keeps growing. You also don't walk to the top of the mountain and gaze out at the rolling hills—some snowcapped, some not, luscious greens in different shades that form a beautiful landscape as the sun kisses your skin and the breeze tickles you in a comforting hug—and go "nah, it's just too much." You take in the beauty, you adore the greatness of it.

There is no such thing as too much.

It's an idea that you put into your head. Go back to Chapter 2 and redo the inner child work around this idea of being too much. What happened to you as a child when you were told you were too much? Can you give that version of you the love and appreciation it wanted?

Playwork: Draw a line down the middle of a page in your journal. On the left side write 'my not enoughness' and on the right side write 'my too muchness'. Make a list of the areas in your life you feel lacking and on the other side the areas in your life that you feel like you aren't deserving to be you in. See what comes up

After writing this list, look back at it and question why you believe you are not good enough or too much. Do the inner child loving playwork on what comes up.

I mention self-worth in this chapter on pleasure because feeling worthy feels really, really good. Self-worth feels like an internal fire has been lit and your inner bully has turned into your biggest fan and is constantly cheering you on. *Feeling good feels really good.*

**WHEN YOU FEEL GOOD
YOU LOOK GOOD.**

**WHEN YOU THINK GOOD
YOU LOOK GOOD.**

**WHEN YOU SAY GOOD
YOU LOOK GOOD.**

**WHEN YOU DO GOOD
YOU LOOK GOOD.**

**WHEN YOU EAT GOOD
YOU LOOK GOOD.**

**WHEN YOU SLEEP GOOD
YOU LOOK GOOD.**

**WHEN YOU LOVE YOUR LIFE
YOU LOOK GOOD.**

Setting Yourself Up for Success

How would you feel if you knew you could start each day feeling amazing about yourself and totally vibing with your life? That is what I call setting yourself up for success, aka your morning routine.

At the beginning of this chapter you made a list of things that brought you pleasure. From this list you can now start to create a morning routine that will put you into a 'yes and Yes and YES' state.

My morning routine has me doing things that I know will put me in a feel-great state. From that feel-great state I feel empowered, I feel unstoppable, I ooze joy, I start my day with a 'I can do this' attitude. Setting myself up for success is non-negotiable in my life. I'm more productive, I meet more people, I coach better, I have more ideas flowing to me when I feel good. And we know by now that feeling good is a choice! Why would you not want to set yourself up for success?

We get busy, it doesn't take priority in our lives, we are more concerned about others (kids, partner, boss, etc.). Our beliefs get in the way thinking we can't set the time aside for ourselves. If there is ONE thing this book can teach you let it be that your number one priority in life should be to feel great. Go and do the things that make you feel great.

I'll share with you what my current morning routine looks like *only* if you don't start comparing yours to mine; remember that this is *individual,* my pleasure might not be the same as yours. If checking your WhatsApp in the morning to listen to a voice note from your best friend feels great to you, then do that. If making a cup of coffee feels so comforting and just a 'YES' in the morning, then do that. There are no rules to what you can or cannot do to make you feel great, and you are the only person who knows what feeling great to you feels like.

Sidenote: I'm a big believer in non-violence; when I say do what makes you feel great, I mean do what makes you feel great that is non-harmful to others or to yourself. I had to put this in here as I suddenly had a thought: what if bullying people makes them feel great? Ultimately any act of violence where there is physical violence or non-physical violence comes from a deep internal feeling of lack. It usually stems from needing to feel better than or proving (usually to themselves) that they are indeed worthy. So go and do what feels great for you as long as there is no harm involved. If you do have tendencies towards violence and this could include bullying, self-harm or eating disorders I suggest you reach out to a professional who can hold the space for you to uncover what is truly going on underneath.

What my (current) morning routine looks like (timings are just rough estimates):

6:30 – 7:30 a.m. Wake up with my affirmations playing as my alarm

7:30 a.m. Go for a run if I feel like it

8:00 a.m. Swim in the pool to cool down, make myself some herbal tea or matcha (depending if I'm detoxing or not)

8:30 a.m. Sit down in front of my altar, play my meditation song, draw my cards, then meditate for approx. 30 min

9:30 a.m. Shower and get ready whilst listening to Abraham Hicks

10:00 a.m. Do my mindset journalling, sometimes whilst eating breakfast

11-ish Start my work

Some days I have client calls at 8:00 a.m. and I don't do all this in this order. Other days I don't even do any of this. Some days I don't meditate till about 2:00 p.m. The point being I naturally tend to gravitate towards wanting to do at least some of these activities because *I know it makes me feel great*. In fact when I don't do it I crave it.

Playwork: Set up a morning routine for yourself where the focus is to get yourself feeling better and better and better.

I'll break down my morning routine for you so you get an insider look at the reasons why I do what I do. I wake up with my affirmations playing on my Amazon Echo dot. I used to reach for my phone to check the time and although it was always on airplane mode, that same act of reaching for my phone and looking at the screen would make me want to check my social media, the urge being so strong! Now I turn my phone off using Screen Time and it doesn't turn on until 11:00 a.m., sometimes even later.

If I wake up and feel like going for a run I will. I listen to my body as I now trust it, something I have had to develop over the years. Exercise is a non-negotiable in my life; I exercise at least once a day, if not twice. It reconnects me back to my body and I get to feel grateful at the strength and resilience that I have.

Always before I sit down for meditation I'll drink a big glass of water or have some lemon water or drink my matcha (depends on whether I am fasting or detoxing). I have a mini ritual when it comes to preparing myself to drop into my meditation. I always start by playing the same song. I've been playing the song for around two years. The song is 'Ong Namo' by Snatam Kaur. As the song plays I light my two candles and my sage as well as my Palo Santo. I draw a card as I ask my question for the day and then sit down and sing my heart out to my song. This song reconnects me back to myself and reconnects me to the energies of the universe every single time I play it. Towards the end of my meditation I'll always add some NLP towards my goals or just run through what I want in my life. This gets me excited about being a conscious creatress of my reality and *I get to feel the feelings NOW* of having achieved those goals without them actually being materialised.

As I get ready I pop on some Abraham Hicks videos from YouTube; I just love Abraham because I resonate with what they say and I'm usually laughing or having these big aha moments in my shower, as well as listening to them being such a great reminder that *we can choose how we feel.*

My mindset journalling is my newest addition to my morning routine. I used to journal a lot before; however, mindset journalling is more specific as it really gets you into the state of feeling how you want to feel. It's about asking yourself the right kinds of questions so that you start to embody that woman who has everything you want already.

I compiled a list of some of my favourite mindset journalling questions so you could experience for yourself how amazing this practice is.

Playwork: Go and download my PDF of feel-great mindset journalling questions to use daily.

Find the PDF here:
www.norawendel.com/confidentsexyfree

i decide my vibe

Now the thing about your morning routine is that you've got to do it. It's no use planning a beautiful morning routine and then not doing it. Remember that the whole idea and purpose of creating this feel-good morning routine for yourself is for you to ... *feel really good.* Can you make the commitment to yourself that you are going to do it *more often than not* to set yourself up for success?

This doesn't give you permission to beat yourself up when you don't do your morning routine. Notice how I use the phrase 'more often than not' in the paragraph above. That phrase in itself gives you permission to not *have* to do your morning routine every single day; however, the idea is that you want to be doing it more times than you don't do it. There is no number to what that means. It's a phrase I use with myself often as it allows my inner bully to keep quiet.

~

This chapter has really been about getting you to prioritise pleasure in your life to allow yourself to feel good. I really want to emphasise that when you feel good everything around you starts to get better and better. There's a great saying that I love and it goes something like this: "The better you feel, the better you feel."

You understand the power of that, don't you?

Pleasure isn't just sexual pleasure; being attuned to pleasure is an inner awakening of the richness that life has to offer us, it's a tantalising of the senses, it's an acknowledgement and welcoming of your feminine receiving and it just feels so damn good. Go and be a pleasure priestess and spread this idea far and wide!

In the next chapter I'll be unravelling why we are so afraid to be ourselves, why judgment scares us and what jealousy really means. Fear, judgments and jealousy are all things that are stopping you from being fully you. It's time to own Who You Are.

*YOU WILL
NEVER
INFLUENCE
THE WORLD
BY TRYING
TO BE LIKE IT*

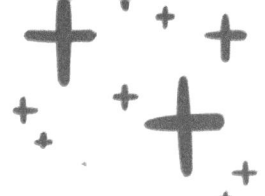

chapter 6
it's safe to be me

It's so easy to 'think' I'm just going to be me, do me. And yet how many times have you truly just let yourself go without doubting yourself? Not many, I bet. Why is that? Why are we so afraid to just be ourselves? This is one of my favourite topics to discuss and question myself in. Why do I fear being myself so much? Welcome to Chapter 6, understanding your fears around showing up and letting go of that fear.

What does it even mean to be yourself?

Authenticity is a word used often to describe someone who is truly themselves. It's another one of those overused words, especially in the coaching industry, that has me roll my eyes; however, it's also a word that people use to describe me, so let's deconstruct authenticity to lead us into uncovering how you can be more you.

What Is Authenticity and What Are the Qualities of an Authentic Person?

I describe authenticity as someone who is connected to themselves, does the inner work to know their own triggers, shows up in integrity with their values and does what they say they will do.

I am no different in how I show up online to how I am in person. I'm clear with my desires, I am not afraid to express them even if it's uncomfortable. I feel reliable, open, true to Nora. It's an attractive quality to have. We all have had a friend who totally did something out of the blue that was out of character that made us question who that person really was. No one wants to be friends or hang out with someone who is flaky and unreliable; it's no fun and it feels like you end up taking responsibility for them.

Authenticity means having an open mind and being willing to listen to other people.

Authenticity means knowing your values and believing in them (and being open to changing them if you need).

Authenticity means having a high level of self-awareness (also known as emotional intelligence).

Authenticity means being able to express yourself and getting your needs met.

Authenticity means being kind to yourself and to others around you.

Yes, authenticity means you have to know who you are.

Some of the women I work with feel like they don't know who they are. If you grew up in a strong religious environment, if you had parents who imposed their dreams on you or if you just followed what everybody else did you may be feeling the disconnect from yourself.

Connection to self is glazed over in modern society which prides itself on action (which is also why we feel not enough, *there will always be more to do*! It's the feeling of never being able to keep up, it's a horrible feeling.). This is also why it seems like there is never enough time. "Time's running out, I'm getting older. If I don't have children now ... I'm too old to start this ..." Those are all beliefs that are coming from low self-worth. It's the hamster wheel of pressure to DO NOW. Even just writing this makes me feel anxious about not being good enough!

If you never give yourself time to just BE, you'll never have the chance to feel into who you are. Since our society prides itself on action, we *feel* we have to keep doing, doing, doing. It doesn't leave space for the BEING.

If you are struggling with figuring out who you are, what you like, what you want or what your purpose is, allow yourself some time to just be. It doesn't have to be a whole year, although I know some of you have done that. It can be an hour a week. Don't schedule anything, not even reading (reading fills your mind too). Allow your intuition to guide you into what you want to be doing, or 'non-doing', aka being.

Here in Bali there is a day of the year called Nyepi. It's the Balinese New Year and it's become my favourite day because the whole island shuts down. No flights coming in or out, most shops and cafes close, we are meant to stay at home, not speak and not use light at night. It's the most peaceful day. When the whole island goes into peace mode there is a different energy in the air; it feels potent with possibility, it feels deeply rejuvenating. It's the one day a year I allow myself to do absolutely nothing. Last year I sat for four hours and stared at the rice fields drinking herbal tea whilst I had the most amazing ideas flow into my mind (I didn't even write them down as that would have been doing something). I felt like I was in a bliss bubble of 'me-ness'. This year I sat on my balcony and watched the birds and the trees and felt this overwhelming sense of abundance all around me. Again that feeling of surrendering into life, life without having to prove anything.

Nyepi makes such a big impact on me as (sadly) it's the only day I don't feel like I have to get on with my to-do list! Because of Nyepi and how it made me reconnect back to being Nora, I now bring more and more pockets of 'being Nora' time into my weekly schedule.

Playwork: Try scheduling one hour this week to do absolutely nothing. Notice what comes up

Being is also a part of the feminine. Doing is part of the masculine. Scheduling 'you' time without distractions is one way to fine-tune your radar to find your purpose, to understand yourself without external influence and to get more comfortable just being you.

Another great way to figure out who you really are is by asking yourself the right questions. Try these below:

What do I like?
What makes me feel good?
What do I want?
Why do I want that?
Why don't I have it yet?
What are my beliefs stopping me?
What childhood experience made me internalise that belief?
Why am I making it difficult on myself?

How can I make my life easier?
How can I be my own best friend?
What do I really need right now?
Why am I afraid?

You've been answering these questions in some form or another throughout this whole book already. These are personal development questions that are guiding you towards getting to know yourself more. There is no right or wrong way to answer these questions and you can answer them as many times as you like throughout your whole life.

We as humans automatically strive for growth, for betterment, to be able to live our highest potential. It's when this striving becomes twisted from a place of feeling not good enough or lacking in or needing to be loved that it turns us into competitive, self-flagellating Pacman humans who just have to keep eating to feel anything remotely like worthiness.

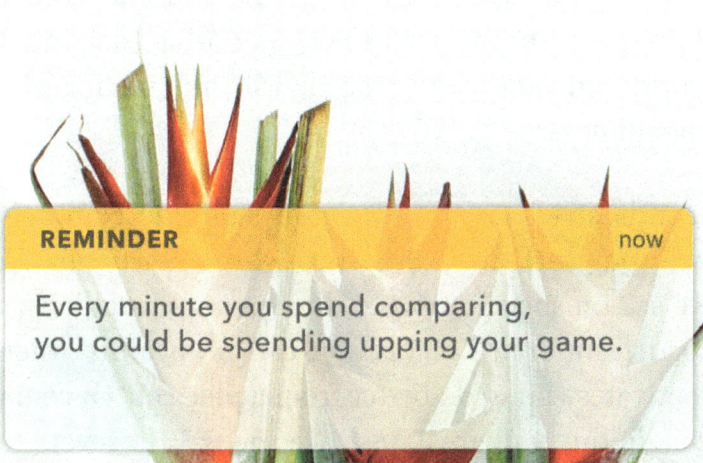

REMINDER now

Every minute you spend comparing,
you could be spending upping your game.

Let me ask you a question: If you were all alone in the most magnificent jungle, it was safe, there was enough food and water for you, there wasn't anyone else around, how would you feel about yourself?

You'd probably feel really good. You wouldn't worry about how she was doing better at plucking fruits than you, wouldn't worry about if you were thin enough to wear that bikini. You'd just be you and go about doing you. Yet this isn't the case. Put us back into the world and there we go again with the feeling of not enoughness.

In this striving for growth we start the comparison with our external influencers which can be anything we see on social media to the woman living down the road from you. Comparison can be healthy when it motivates you to do better from a place of "Of course I can do this, I'm great, just like she is." However, most of us have a chronic case of comparisonitus; we just can't stop comparing ourselves to everyone out there.

I'm not as slim/curvy as she is.
I'm not as extroverted/introverted as she is.
I'm not making as much money as she is.
My relationship isn't as loving as hers is.
I must not be good enough because I don't have as many Instagram followers.

Comparison is inbuilt in us; I suffer from it too. The difference is I don't let it get me down (most of the time). I see it as a way in which I can dive deeper into my desires and figure out what the belief is that is stopping me from having what she has. Go through this set of journalling questions to get more of an idea of why you are comparing, what your beliefs are underneath the comparison and then figure out an action you can take to stop the comparing.

journalling questions

What/who am I comparing myself to?

What do they have that I don't think I have?

Why is it causing me to feel bad about myself?

What beliefs are coming up around this?

How do I want to feel instead?

What can I do to feel that way right now?

Comparing makes us feel terrible; it really digs into that feeling of lack of worth. It's easy enough to keep saying stop comparing, yet the 'how do I stop comparing?' question took me a long time to figure out.

When you realise that you can have anything you want then when you feel that icky feeling of comparison it's a chance for you to see that you want what she has. I talked about Abraham Hicks and how contrast is part of life and it's here to show us what we do want by also showing us what we don't want.

Start looking at comparison that way too; it's simply a chance for you to navigate towards more of what you do want in your life. And if you are still saying I don't know what I do want and at the same time you've got comparisonitus, make a list of all the things you have been comparing and there you have your list of what you do want.

Comparison in this way, when it comes from a feeling of lack of self-worth, is ultimately competition; it's your belief that you can't have it, it's either/or. She can have it, I can't have it. Do you think it would be possible for you to turn that around and see it as we can all have it;

if she can have it, so can I, if it's possible for her, it's possible for me?

Feel good belief: If it's possible for her, it's possible for me.

Let's talk about jealousy. Jealousy is a low vibration feeling. Jealousy is you thinking she has something that *I* can't have; it's similar to comparison! I want you to think about the last time you were jealous. Why were you jealous? What caused you to be jealous? What did they have that you really wanted that you thought you couldn't have?

There really is no need for jealousy when you start to feel into the idea that you can have it all. The same way as you can use comparison to guide you towards more of what you want, you can also use the feeling of jealousy as your emotional navigational system guiding you more and more towards what you want and who you want to be.

If you get my gist you'll start to notice that I don't believe there are any "bad" feelings in this world; there are feelings we don't like and there are feelings that we do like and want more of. I am highly aware of my feelings and how they *make me feel* and I'm constantly using how I feel to create the life that I do want to live.

Why Do We Fear Being Ourselves?

This still leaves us with the question of why do we fear being our full selves? What is it that stops you from just being you? The answer to this question came to me after I had integrated and healed my anxiety. I had anxiety because ***I didn't feel safe.*** It was such a big realisation when I saw that I felt like I couldn't fully express myself because *I didn't feel safe expressing myself.*

Safety for women is a huge subject and I'm just going to be addressing one part of this, the part that had the biggest impact on me. When a woman feels safe she blossoms. That feeling of safety is different for everyone; let's dig into what safety means for you.

journalling questions

What does safety mean for me?

What makes me feel safe?

Where am I not feeling safe in my life right now?

What can I do to feel safe in those areas?

You're feeling like you can't be you because it's not safe to be you and it's not safe to express who you are. This feeling would have come from your childhood; perhaps you were told it wasn't okay to do what you wanted to do, maybe you have a fear of Doing It Wrong, maybe you have a fear of rejection.

All of these lead back to the same thing: ***you want to be loved.***

If you want to get over this fear of self-expression it's a great practice to start asking yourself what is going to happen if I do it? What is the worst-case scenario? Allow yourself to go down those ideas in your head until you reach the darkest fault and it often leads to your deepest fear. That is also why it feels so damn scary. I want you to use this process to uncover what your deepest fear is around expressing yourself.

journalling questions

What do I think is going to happen if I do it?

and if I do it then what will happen?

and then after that what will happen
and how will I feel?

and then?

and then?

and then?

Once you get the deep-rooted fear you can objectively look at it and ask yourself *is it really that bad?* Is that really what's going to happen? More often than not when you bring the deep-rooted fear to the surface it fades away or at least you can break down the fear until it doesn't feel so scary anymore.

At the same time as you are unravelling that deep-rooted scary fear, you're asking yourself what would make it safe to actually express myself (or take the action you really want to).

For example, say I wanted to go to ecstatic dance and just let loose, not giving a f*ck about anyone else (I've got some emotions to release!), yet I feel like I just can't do it.

I'm worried about how I look, I'm worried I can't dance, I'm worried people will stare at me and judge me ...

Going through those journalling questions, I realise I want to dance freely and I don't feel like I can, if I do dance I'll look like an idiot, people will laugh at me, I'll feel ashamed, I won't be liked, no one will be my friend, I'll be all alone, I'll get sad.

That's my thought process.

If I think about what would make me feel safe to dance I come up with several things: having my friends dance with me, dancing at the back of the space, choosing not to care, first going to smaller ecstatic dances to feel more comfortable.

I can then decide how I want to act based on my realisations above. Doing this clears some space within me of frustration and I can then move forward with self-compassion instead of self-hate.

Your turn to take yourself through this exact same process. Ask yourself what is going to happen if you do what you really fear! What's the worst-case outcome? How do you want to feel instead? What can you do to feel safe?

It's so empowering

to say

"This isn't serving me."

and walk away in peace.

Setting Boundaries (Especially With Family!)

Often we fear being ourselves because we are conscious of what our family might think. I know I often think about that and it stops me from doing what I want to do, which leads to me being frustrated as I can't express myself, which then leads to me being hard on myself for not feeling like I can express myself, which then leads me to not feel good. Argh, I hate that cycle!

Family matters (to most of us) because it's where our direct source of love came from when we were children. The idea that doing something to upset that source of love (even when we are adults) is frightening. What can you do about it?

When a family member messages me or talks to me (aka shares their opinion) about my work or how I am living my life, I listen to their opinion and I notice the feelings that arise in my body. Sometimes it's shame, sometimes it's anger; I pay attention, I choose to not react immediately and then I reply to them, *"I get that you think that, thank you for sharing that with me."*

I don't argue or talk back; if anything at all, I say, "I don't want to discuss this." I set my own boundaries in place because I know talking more about this will trigger and deeply upset me and the family member I am dealing with. By saying "Thank you for sharing, I get that you think that," it's an *acknowledgement of their being and their opinion*. It doesn't mean I have to take it on and at the same time I am not dismissing them and their right to their own life viewpoint.

I also remind myself that everyone is showing up in this life with their own set of stories, their own sets of beliefs and their own childhood core wounds running who they think they can be or who they think other people can be. When I have a conversation or even an argument with close friends or family members I always remind myself that they have their own inner issues. It's never personal. This is a great way to put things into perspective (especially if you are a chronic people pleaser).

Whenever I am triggered by someone else's opinion or reaction to me, I recognise that my reaction is coming from my longing to want to be loved. I do want love (we all do) and *I do want validation* (especially from my dad; I feel that very strongly, even today) and that it feels edgy for me to say no and yet by saying no I am stepping fully into my own power and with that comes the freedom to be me. It takes practice to stand up for yourself because our natural tendency is to stay safe and protected within our 'tribe'; saying NO feels like saying no to our tribe. That's not the case; saying no means you value yourself. I suggest to start saying no to small things that won't cause a huge internal fear trigger in you. Say no to going out with friends one night if you just want to stay at home; say no to second servings when you feel stuffed at the dinner table.

Feel good belief: It's safe to be me. It's safe to want what I want. It's safe to say no.

One of my closest friends once told me that the more I say no to her the more that she can trust my YES. Saying yes when you don't really mean it is a watered-down yes. I know I'd rather be with people who actually WANT to be with me rather than them doing it out of guilt or FOMO or any other lack ideas. *Be strong in your nos and then your yeses will be even stronger.*

journalling questions:

Where am I letting my boundaries get loose?

What can I say no to that's not working for me right now?

What are my big F YESES?

~

How are you feeling about being more of you right now? Empowered? Still a little fearful?

I have a challenge for you: post something on Instagram stories you've always wanted to post about and have felt scared to do. Use the processes in this chapter to give you the courage to do it. Maybe you'll share more of your personal story, maybe you'll dance on camera (not for anyone but for yourself!), maybe you'll share some of your work. Do it! You'll feel so proud once you do.

Tag me on Instagram @norawendel and use the hashtag #confidentsexywildlyfree so I can see and celebrate you!

people will love
you

people will hate
you

and none of it
will have
anything to do
with you.

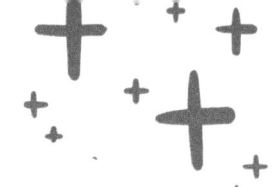

chapter 7
self + other

We just learnt and unpacked the role that safety plays in the ability to feel like you can just be you. In this chapter I'll share some tools based on Authentic Relating that will allow you to start expressing even more of who you are. It's these tools that will allow you to become that wildly free woman, where freedom means the choice to do, be, have, express anything you desire.

Up until now you've seen that your desire to be loved governs all your actions; when we aren't aware of this underlying need to be loved it turns into manipulation, neediness, feelings of lack, competitiveness, perfectionism and so forth. The reason I fell in love with Authentic Relating when I first experienced it in Cape Town was that *I felt seen* and feeling seen is akin to getting the recognition that you matter.

It felt like relief *(I don't have to try so hard anymore)*.
It felt like understanding *(I don't need to prove anymore)*.
It felt freeing *(I don't need to be anyone else but me)*.

In the beginning of this book I shared that as children we want to be seen, heard and appreciated. We want to

be validated in our existence. That need still continues into adulthood and we spend our lives not knowing that validation via love is what we want. We think it's status we want or the newest iPhone or man, when in fact it's all leading back to "look at me, recognise me; *tell me I matter.*"

It's the same with purpose: we long to know our purpose because then we feel like we *matter* in this world and we have something to *contribute*. I remember feeling so small when I lived in New Delhi and had my second major bout of anxiety. I had a jewellery company making yoga jewellery and it felt so unfulfilling. I didn't know why and I couldn't decide what I did want. This made me feel lacklustre, panicky and worthless, all feelings which increased my anxiety. It wasn't a great time of my life. Finding my purpose took 10 years, and still today I'm not sure I have a 'final' purpose (maybe we all have many!). Don't stress yourself out and let your inner bully tell you you are worthless because you haven't found the ONE THING you are meant to do. Do the things that feel great to you and you won't worry about that anymore. Navigate towards pleasure (you can call it joy or happiness) and finding your purpose will naturally follow suit. It has to! We are conditioned to play roles in society, finding that job to secure the income to then buy the house, yet if it doesn't make you happy, what is the point? Don't get confused with letting other people's happiness interfere with your own internal feeling of happiness.

Purpose will come once you follow what makes you feel alive, on fire, excited and joyful. Keep following that aliveness.

That's what I learnt to do and today my life is amazing. I feel great, I have the tools to navigate my emotions so I can constantly fine-tune my life towards more and more of the feel-good feelings, I understand the unlimited potential of what I can have (anything!) *and I get to be me.*

By being me in all the ways I also get to inspire other women to be themselves too.

We all need someone to look up to adoringly and go, "Wow, that's possible? Right on! I want some of that in my life!" Forget the competition, unhealthy comparison and jealousy, use other women (and men) to inspire you into *your greatness.*

Feel good belief: I get to be me.

Feel good belief: Feeling great is my #1 priority.

I'M FUCKING SPECIAL

The Foundation of Authentic Relating

The reason I share about Authentic Relating in this book is because relationships are the basis of our lives and society at large. We have a multitude of relationships from our family relationships, to our friends, to our coworkers, to the person at the supermarket checkout, to our love partners. Relationships are everywhere; we don't live in a mono society. The word itself—society—means people living together. We aren't monks or nuns who give up our worldly life to go and turn inwards in mountain caves or jungles. How we create, nurture and operate in our relationships matter, and the crazy part? No one teaches us how to have beautiful, nourishing relationships!

Think back to your relationships (include all the different ones). How did they start? How did they end? Were your needs met? Were you hurt? Did they thrive?

The most important and life-changing relationship is the relationship you have with yourself. If you don't create and nurture this one, you'll never live a life where you feel worthy, confident in yourself or feel free to be, do or have whatever you desire.

Authentic Relating teaches self-realisation through social 'games' or practices that you play with others. You get to know more of who you are in relation to the other; at the same time you learn how to create nurturing and thriving relationships.

Authentic Relating teaches you emotional intelligence (how to understand your emotions), how to be a great listener, how to express your emotions, how to hold space non-judgmentally and how to create the relationships that allow your needs to be met.

Authentic Relating taught me how to express myself without the fear of being rejected, abandoned or ashamed to be me.

I can't teach you the intricacies of Authentic Relating as it's a practice to be experienced and felt. I can, however, share with you some foundational principles and some of the practices you can use to learn how to express yourself better. Authentic Relating International is the organisation that I trained with and they lead Authentic Relating nights worldwide (google Authentic Relating + your location to find if there are Authentic Relating events near you). Take a step into this world and you'll understand the power of being seen, appreciated and how beautiful it feels to be able to be your wild, weird, wacky self.

The three foundational principles of Authentic Relating that helped me to start expressing myself more are:

1. **Welcome everything**
2. **Assume nothing**
3. **Reveal your experience**

Authentic Relating Principle 1: Welcome Everything

Just like this book has taught you, there are no right or wrong feelings, every feeling you have is valid precisely because it is your experience. Some experiences we categorise as 'good' and others as 'bad'. It's through Authentic Relating I saw that I was trying to deny my 'bad' feelings, my inner bully punching me and telling me I was not a good person for feeling those feelings; it was leading me into a spiral of self-hate. Examples of my bad feelings were being scared to go outside my home, feeling ashamed for having anxiety and lacking confidence, etc.

Welcome everything means you want to welcome all your feelings, no need to categorise, simply observe them for what they are. Welcome everything you are feeling by saying to yourself, "Oh I feel this right now (don't create a story around it!), oh and now I feel this ... How interesting!"

Ask yourself:

- **What am I feeling right now?**
- **And now?**
- **And now?**

Simply naming your feelings often dissipates them quicker, especially those we categorise as 'not good'— anger, fear, shame, guilt, etc. Welcome, acknowledge, breathe and repeat. A feeling will fade if you don't dramatise it.

NO ONE HAS THEIR SHIT TOGETHER

Authentic Relating Principle 2:
Assume Nothing

The second principle, assume nothing, is pivotal in changing your perspective about life and other people. I was the queen of assumptions. I assumed everyone knew more than me and that I was being left out; it made me feel resentful, ashamed and small. The irony here is that we all go around thinking people know what's going on in our heads (at least some of it). That's false; if I stand in front of you I can guess (assume) your mood by your body language and facial expression. I can't, however, read your mind. It's only when you open your mouth and *tell me how you feel* or what's going on for you that I can be a part of your world. If you don't share with me how you truly feel, it's me assuming I know how you feel. Assumptions are the number one relationship killer, by the way!

We go about life assuming that we aren't liked, that the man we want may reject us or that we can't earn the money we want. Our assumptions are stopping us from getting what we want. We don't know if it's true or not until we either a) do it or b) ask clarifying questions.

Stop assuming, take action or ask to know more!

journalling question

What are my biggest assumptions about myself, my life and the people around me?

Assumptions and beliefs are tied together because *we assume* that our beliefs are true! We don't question them and this means our beliefs rule our lives and we wonder why we aren't getting what we want. Duh! Start questioning your assumptions and start questioning your beliefs. *Is this really true? Is this what I want to be believing? Is this working for me?* are some of the questions you can ask yourself.

Assumptions don't allow us to be open-minded. Open-mindedness is a part of being authentic and we need to stay open if we want to grow, thrive and experience new things in our lives (all of which are outside of our comfort zone, by the way). The easiest way to stop assuming and to keep an open mind is to look at the world as if it's *your first time experiencing any of it.*

I like to take the example of a child; children don't assume as much as adults do. They constantly ask clarifying questions so they can start to make sense of the world and form their own identity. A child approaches the world with wonder and awe, always inspired by what's happening around them. Can you approach your life with wonder and awe?

journalling question

What would my life be like if I allowed myself to see the world like a child again, with so much wonder and awe?

This isn't only a journalling question, you can put it into embodied practice. As soon as you put down this book, open your eyes like it's the first beautiful time you are seeing this world. Notice how there is so much to explore and the world becomes exciting, inspiring and playful again. There really is no such thing as boredom when you decide to live life always intrigued, wondering, open and in awe of everything and everyone around you. Apply this to people as well—next time you sit at a cafe, notice your assumptions about people; turn the assumptions into curiosity! Open your energy field by being curious; you'll be amazed at how people start to talk to you as well.

Authentic Relating Principle 3: Revealing Your Experience

Revealing your experience means sharing what is going on for you; if you are able to share your experience (aka your feelings and how they are impacted by the moment), this is when real connection and deeper intimacy can flourish in your relationships, no matter if it is your love relationship, work relationship, friend relationship or family relationship. We often get stuck trying to express ourselves because it feels scary to truly share how we feel. We constantly question ourselves revolving around the same fear of *"If I share, am I threatening the possibility of being loved?"*

Here are four ways you can start revealing your experiences to those around you ...

- **"Right now I am feeling ..."**
- **"Being with you right now I feel ..."**
- **"Hearing you say that makes me feel ..."**
- **"What you said impacted me in this way ..."**

Please understand that you will never be able to get your needs met if you aren't able to ask for them to be met. First it's always finding out what your needs are; often it's as simple as asking yourself:

"What do I need right now?"

The next step is to then be able to ask for it. If it involves another person be prepared that they might not be able to meet your needs; you still have permission to ask for them to be met though! This is the scariest step as you may come across your fear that you won't be loved if you ask for what we need.

If you don't ask, you definitely won't get your needs met.

Sharing what you want/need/desire and feeling safe to do so takes practice and it gets easier each time. Here is how I approach the conversation with someone when I notice I desire something:

"I'm noticing in me a desire to _____. It involves _____ from you. Do you think that is possible?"

Or

"I feel I need _____ from you _____. Are you available for me in that manner right now? If not, what is possible for you?"

If you have a need that can be self-satisfied then great! Give it to yourself, no reason to punish yourself. Yes, that's something we love doing too, thinking we need to hold out on feeling good about ourselves.

Go and practise these tools for authentic expression. It may feel scary but you can do it anyway. Tell your inner child that you got her and you can do scary things together.

Look at you, ==glowing with self-love== and becoming a magnet to good vibrations. ==I'm proud of you.==

Being in tune with your feelings is key to living a life in alignment with your desires. Being able to express how you are feeling is key to getting your needs met which allows you to feel happy, safe, calm, at peace and loved. You getting your needs met is *you doing you*; it doesn't mean you are selfish, it doesn't mean you have to feel guilty when you don't put others first, it doesn't mean you don't care deeply about your friends/family/love. *It's you taking care of the relationship to yourself.* When your needs aren't met you feel angry, frustrated, anxious and fearful. That's not how I want to feel in my life, and I'm sure you don't either.

I want to end this chapter with a few journalling questions that will allow you to examine your current relationships to then allow you to make the conscious decision to change the relationship if it isn't working and benefiting you.

journalling questions

What is my current relationship to myself?

How do I want it to feel?

What can I change to having a more nourishing and thriving relationship to myself?

What relationships are currently working for me? And why is that the case?

What relationships are not working for me? Why is that?

How do I want my love/work/friend relationships to feel?

How can I show up differently in these relationships to allow them to flourish?

Really tune into the feelings you want to feel in your relationships; it's always about choosing how you want to feel and then knowing how your actions can align to create those feelings.

Let's bring all we learnt together in the next chapter where I'll share with you about truly cultivating your confidence, how to own your worth and feel like the badass woman that you are. Ready?

CONFIDENCE IS NOT "THEY WILL LIKE ME"
CONFIDENCE IS "I'LL BE FINE IF THEY DON'T"

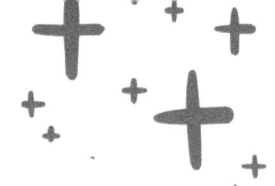

chapter 8
confidence, worth and owning it

It's time to bring it all together. You made it this far, wasn't that a blast? Let's end this book with a big smile on your face, you getting your dancing shoes out of the dusty cupboard and applying that fav lippy of yours. Get it woman. It's your time to own who you are!

Cultivating Confidence

What is confidence? Are you just born with it? Can you wake up one day and suddenly be confident? I'll be answering all that below.

Confidence is a *feeling*, it's an internal feeling of "I got this"; I translate it as the self-belief that you can do anything and even if it doesn't work out the way you wanted it to, you can handle the outcome. Having confidence is life changing (overconfidence leads to being egotistical, narcissistic and being a bitch); when you have confidence you don't let life stop you, hurdles appear and you simply love yourself up, forgive yourself and others if they are involved, and keep going and going and going ...

Confidence *can* be cultivated; it's a muscle to strengthen, you already know some things you can do that make you confident: do more of those things! Step a tiny, tiny bit outside your comfort zone, an area one of my mentors Rick Smith calls 'The Tender Edge', where you can have one foot inside your comfort zone and the other foot just over that boundary where you can explore new things and still feel safe.

Confidence is a great feeling and we want more of those feel-good feelings!

journalling question
What makes me feel confident?

I have a list of things I love doing which makes me feel confident, from dancing to wearing sexy lacy lingerie under my clothes and knowing I have the support of friends. Confidence is personal and I suggest getting clear on what you already do that cultivates that inner feeling of "Yes, I got this!", and then it's a matter of expanding that list slowly and lovingly.

Confidence is sexy. You want to be around someone who is confident (from the heart, not ego confident); they make you feel better. The energy of confidence is also inspiring.

Confidence gets amplified when you have self-worth. Self-worth is the belief that you are enough no matter what you look like, how you behave or what anybody thinks of you. We saw that our idea of worth is interwoven with the idea of achievement which is based on the actions we take (or don't take). Thinking you need to achieve something to feel worth will never lead to worth; it's the opposite. Feeling your worth will lead to *everything* you do being an achievement that makes you feel great!

If you are still feeling that 'not enoughness', go back to Chapter 2 and be kind to yourself as you look through your childhood to understand who told you you weren't worthy. Forgive them, release it, love yourself up, navigate to the things that do make you feel good and keep doing those things. That's the formula for finding your worth.

Stop trying to prove yourself; proving yourself is exhausting. You're only trying to prove to yourself that you are worthy of love. No one outside of yourself will give you your worth.

Feel good belief: I am worthy of love.

Repeat this new belief again and again.

What Is Self-Doubt?

Self-doubt happens when you don't believe you are good enough and are not confident with who you are to achieve what you want to achieve. It's an uneasy feeling of constantly questioning everything that goes through your head (that's your inner bully right there.) Your self-doubt is what is stopping you from what you want in life. We aren't born with doubt, it's instilled in us; look at children, they think they can climb the highest tree branch and they go for it! As adults our life experience and our 'mistakes' either harden the belief that we are not good enough or then motivate us to do better. Which do you do?

If your inner bully is still beating you up, especially around showing up as your fullest self, (posting truthfully on FB, doing a live video on social media, applying for that job you want, quitting your job to start your own business), I want you to challenge it head on. **Doubt your doubt.**

This is how I want you to challenge your inner bully: *So what if I apply for that job that you don't think I am talented enough for? What if I'm the perfect person they are looking for? What if they hire me on the spot? What if they offer me more than the salary they said? What if I have the best colleagues? What if I learn the most from this job? What if I get promoted in six months? ...*

Do you get the gist?

Instead of letting negative Nancy rule your life, play the positive *what if* game. The negative *what if* game leads you into the dungeons of despair; that's no fun and certainly doesn't feel good. The positive *what if* game gets you excited; you can make up endless possibilities. Just ask yourself what would feel really good and be epic if it happened!

Playwork: Play the positive *What If* game to calm your inner bully

darling
just
fucking
own it

Owning It

Confidence and worth both lead to the idea of "I'm hot shit", "I've got this down", aka owning it. Owning it is about accepting yourself as you are whilst still being open to positive growth. You don't want to be the know-it-all or become stagnant. Life is about growth, after all.

Owning it is saying to yourself, *"This is me, and I am amazing!"* Owning it is being proud of who you are, flaws, imperfections, feelings ... everything. It's you honouring yourself.

One day I decided to make an altar to myself. I had an altar for money, an altar for beauty, an altar to my parents, why didn't I have one dedicated to me? My Nora altar contains photos of me (I have a fun polaroid camera I use), it has objects which have meaning to me, my favourite crystals and a candle. It's my reminder of how awesome I am and every time I pass by the altar, I acknowledge myself and feel good about myself.

Playwork: Make an altar dedicated to your awesome self

Not owning yourself is disempowering. Do you say anything along these lines (all of which are disempowering yourself): *"It wasn't me, oh, it's nothing, I don't want to take the credit ..."*? Maybe you are thinking that if you own it, you'll be a bad person or you'll feel guilty for being a good person. It's time to own who you are. Use this journalling question to see where you can empower yourself right now by claiming your awesomeness.

this chapter feels really good.

journalling question
Where can I own it in my life right now?

Owning it means you get to live your fullest life with integrity and no regrets. I don't believe in regret, I only get to learn from what didn't work out the way I wanted it to. Accept that things will happen that aren't the way you wished and be okay with yourself knowing you will overcome them (confidence and worth right there!).

How can you own even more of who you are? Become your own cheerleader in life. Every time you do something go, *"Yes, you are amazing"*, no matter how small.

Got out of bed this morning? "Yes, I'm amazing."
Decided to sleep in? "Yes, I'm amazing."
Posted on Instagram? "Yes, I'm amazing."
Decided not to post on Instagram? "Yes, I'm amazing."

How you talk to yourself matters. If it's constantly negative Nancy on your internal 108.feelbad radio channel you are not going to feel good. Change the channel to 106.feelgood and watch how your external reality will change.

Remember this equation from Chapter 2?

External influence = Thoughts = Beliefs (Belief System) = Behaviour (Action) = Our Reality

If you want to change your reality you have to change how you think. Make the commitment to start talking to yourself like your best friend would: *"You got this, that's easy for you, of course you can do it, I believe in you ..."*

Feel good belief: I rock. I am amazing!

You know that woman on the dance floor who is rocking out without a care in the world? That's her owning who she is. It's magnetic and sexy AF.

Stop Caring What Other People Think of You

When you recognise that you just want to be loved, you'll see that your need for being liked, aka caring what other people think of you, becomes irrelevant. Yes, we all want to be loved. Yes, we all want to matter. Yes, we all want to feel like we belong. It's our human existence. When you are trembling with fear and stuck in inaction because you can't get over the fact that you really, really care about what other people think of you, ask yourself these questions:

journalling questions

Where is this insecurity coming
from?

What will happen if people don't
like me?

How can I do it anyway and be kind
to myself?

Think about the seven billion people in this world.
Are they all going to become sheeple and bow down to
you and sing your praise? Nope. There will always be
people who don't like your message or how you show
up. That's okay. Forgive them, forgive yourself and go
have a party with the people that do like you.

journalling questions

How can I surround myself with the
people that support me?

What can I do to give myself the
love I desire?

This is where boundaries come in; if you know a friend or family member who comments or responds to you in a feel-bad way, you can tell them that this isn't working for you and you don't feel supported, or you can tell them you are no longer available to talk about this topic. That's what I shared with you in Chapter 6. I wasn't willing for my families beliefs to trigger me into a state of self-doubt and not good enoughness! *Do what you have to do to protect yourself from doubting your amazingness.*

GOING WITH THE IDEA THAT NOTHING CAN STOP ME.

What You Really Desire

What is it that you truly desire? You may think you desire the man to feel the love or maybe it's the best girlfriends who you can travel to paradise islands like Bali with …

Is it luxury, 25K cash months or the dress from Topshop that are pinned to your digital vision board?

Is what you desire happiness? Maybe it's self-worth (yep, I know you want that!) and you *definitely* want to feel loved.

It's all the above, AND there is more.

What you as a woman truly desire is **FREEDOM.**

I know deep down there's this desire for *complete freedom in self-expression.*

The freedom to wear whatever, and I mean whatever, you want at any time.
The freedom to walk up to any man and be confident in just saying hello.
The freedom to sexually express yourself.
The freedom to be that crazy woman on the dance floor with a smile so wide it blinds.
The freedom to not care about how you look (daggy, sexy, mum-like or red carpet queen).
The freedom to say f*ck it and just do you.

I know because I had the same desires.

Insecurity was my norm. I constantly doubted myself, my lack of self-worth was akin to me climbing the tallest mountain that never seemed to end—*such a MF struggle.* You've read this book because you have the same feelings:—sucky, shitty, shamey feelings.

You go through phases of being fine, feeling pretty good about yourself and your life and one day you aren't fine. Bed seems like the perfect way to do life since you don't have to see anyone or face anything.

And yet the job calls; you put your pretty makeup face on to look 'fine' and get on with it. Friends make you laugh, wine makes you feel better and throughout it all the underlying niggle of listlessness is never totally gone.

You are not fine.
And you are barely getting 'on' with it.

Freedom is screaming your name and yet you are caged within yourself, scrambling to see if you can fit through the bars. But you can't. Tired of yourself, you sit in the corner and think *"Is this it?"*

"Am I destined to be this awkward, caged, self-hating and doubting all my life?"

No, you are not.

There isn't even a key to find to unlock the cage. It's you who put that cage around yourself.

Once you start the journey towards yourself the struggle fades with it and the cage simply dissolves.

The journey starts with you screaming your head off inside the cage. It's the awareness that you are in a place you don't want to be. You can scream all you want and you know the cage isn't going anywhere, it's your own hard steel lockdown.

As you grow weary of yourself the internal screaming subsides; it's time to start the digging. It's time to find the thoughts you keep thinking which are creating your beliefs and belief systems, which are in turn ruling your external actions, those same external actions which create the very reality of the cold-hearted cage you find yourself in.

You have started to unravel those thoughts of self-hate, self-doubt, self-pity, self-criticising and self-victimising. You have started because you recognise right now that you don't want to feel small, insecure and shy anymore.

You want the freedom to be you in all your fullness, Womaness and aliveness.

What you truly desire is freedom, freedom from yourself to be yourself.

Freedom from the ideas of who you cannot be, because in reality it's only you who is imagining the cage to be real.

~

it's only you who decides who you can or cannot be.

it's only you who decides who you can or cannot be.

it's only you who decides who you can or cannot be.

it's only you who decides who you can or cannot be.

it's only you who decides who you can or cannot be.

it's only you who decides who you can or cannot be.

it's only you who decides who you can or cannot be.

it's only you who decides who you can or cannot be.

it's only you who decides who you can or cannot be.

it's only you who decides who you can or cannot be.

it's only you who decides who you can or cannot be.

it's only you who decides who you can or cannot be.

And there you have it, my 10 years of internal processes, shifts, struggles, anxiety-ridden house-bound days all laid out for you to journey more into your YOUNESS. I told you this wasn't *just* a book. If you read through these pages and didn't do the playwork, I'll give you a hug and ask you again, ***"How badly do you want it?"***

How badly do you want to become a confident, sexy and wildly free woman living a life filled with laughs, friends, luxury and effortlessness?

Because becoming a confident, sexy and wildly free woman is a process, it's a process that starts by knowing what you want and why you don't have it yet. It's about kindly uncovering those stories you tell yourself as you stroke and hold your inner child's hand, promising to never leave her and always love her.

It's about understanding that you want to be loved; oh, how deeply this yearning for love shows up in your life! Stop manipulating yourself to get that love. It's available to you anytime you decide to love yourself first.

It's about reconnecting to the beauty, play and aliveness that being a woman is and welcoming more of you into that space. It's about asking yourself why you are choosing to make it hard on yourself when it can be effortless. Ah, relief! Yes, it does get to be this easy!

It's about your feelings, it's *always about feeling good*. Decide right now that feeling good great is going to be your priority in life and then constantly navigate towards that. No, you are not selfish nor do you need to feel guilty by wanting to feel great. You feeling great gives permission to everyone around you to feel great as well. Be the inspiration.

It's about you standing up for YOU, putting up that red tape around yourself when other people do things that don't work for you, to remind them that you're prioritising you right now.

Becoming a confident, sexy and wildly free woman is about you getting onto that dance floor in your favourite sassy sexy outfit and declaring to the world, THIS IS ME, with the biggest smile on your face, your inner radio tuned to 106.feelgreat and your inner child ecstatically bouncing around you as you bust out those moves, OWNING it and not caring what anyone thinks of you because you know you got this thing called life more than handled.

I told you this was going to be a wild ride into the depths of you. You can take off the helmet now, we've arrived back at yours. *"Same time next week?"* I ask you as I wink and smile my cheeky smile at you, revving my big black sexy motorbike.

"Ready for more?"

Xo
Nora

PS I can't wait to join you on the dance floor.

CONFIDENCE, WORTH AND OWNING IT

more, more, i want more!

Did I just hear you scream that? Okay, okay, no need to make a scene, I got loads more juiciness for you because that's how I live my life—filled up with juicy, feel-great feelings. Don't believe me? Check out my Instagram and send me a voice note into my DMs. I love hearing your voice, 'cause, woman, you matter, so it's time to stand up and speak up. My instagram is @norawendel.

I want you to know that you can read this book again (and again and again) and ask yourself the *same* questions and *do the same playwork*; it never stops, there are always more ways to feel great. There is no end to digging into more of you because what you want changes constantly and that's the beauty of it! Life will always bring contrasts to you and you can always use your feelings to turn towards more greatness in your life.

This book was the beginning of the journey towards more of your confidence, sexiness, aliveness and all around radiance. Want to continue to do this inner work with me? Come and check out my online programs to take this work to the next level. There is always more to uncover around why you are stopping yourself! Check out my latest offerings here: www.norawendel.com/onlinecourses

If you want more of me and my weekly updates on how I view my life and how I deal with my blocks and stories as I grow my coaching business whilst living an effortlessly luxurious and pleasurable life in Bali, come join my newsletter. Every Monday I send out my Monday Motivation newsletter with journalling questions that I am personally using to expand my thoughts. Thursday is Truth Talk Thursday where I share intimate updates on what is happening in my life.

I'm here for you. I'm here dancing away, smiling so big because I can see that life is here to uplift and inspire you even when it feels like it wants you to stay small and shy. It's just another opportunity to ask yourself, *"What do I really want? And why do I think I can't have it?"*

Because the reality is, it's only you who is stopping you.

Big love,
Always, in all the ways.

PS You totally got this.
And yes, the better it gets, the better it gets.

Here's to your awesomeness.

And in between, I found myself.

Stripped of my shame,
my edges slowly softened.

A sigh of relief glistening on my lips.
My eyes closed and body moving.

And in between,
The inhale and exhale.
My seeing and knowing.

I found myself.
Softly enfolded by my own sweetness.

I sat and waited for myself for years,
And it was only in between,

I noticed I was missing.

I have a request. If you were inspired, motivated or straight up loved this book, purchase a copy (or three) to give to your girlfriends. This is the work. This is what life is about, reconnecting to yourself, understanding your desires, figuring out why you think you can't have what you desire, showing up fully as yourself and screaming at the top of your lungs; "I love my life".

Mm yes.
The more we all get to do this, the more others get inspired that they too can have this.

xx

Made in the USA
Las Vegas, NV
15 September 2022